Newmarket Public Library

The Queen

The Queen

· A SCREENPLAY ·

PETER MORGAN

Newmarket Public Library

miramax books

HYPERION

NEW YORK

Copyright © 2006 Peter Morgan

All rights reserved. No part of this book may be used or reproduced in any
manner whatsoever without the written permission of the Publisher.
Printed in the United States of America. For information address
Hyperion, 77 West 66th Street, New York, New York 10023-6298.

ISBN: 1-4013-0903-8
ISBN-13: 978-1-4013-0903-9

Hyperion books are available for special promotions and premiums.
For details contact Michael Rentas, Assistant Director, Inventory Operations,
Hyperion, 77 West 66th Street, 12th floor, New York, New York 10023,
or call 212-456-0133.

Design by Victoria Hartman

MAY 17 2007

FIRST EDITION

1 3 5 7 9 10 8 6 4 2

The Queen

1.   ARCHIVE TELEVISION FOOTAGE

It's Election Day 1997. Up and down the country, the PEOPLE OF BRITAIN, people of all shapes and sizes and denominations, black and white, young and old, are going to the Polls.

Everyone, that is, except the people that live in . . .

2.   EXT. BUCKINGHAM PALACE—DAY

The most instantly recognisable Palace in the world.

The Royal Standard (the flag of heraldic lions and symbolic harp-strings that signals the Monarch's presence), flutters on the roof.

3.   INT. BUCKINGHAM PALACE—CHINESE ROOM DAY

We're in a state room at Buckingham Palace. A TV plays in the corner. (Election footage. We can pick out some of the TV commentary.)

TV COMMENTARY
'. . . here's Tony Blair, "the coming man," "the future" some
have called him, just 43 years old, arriving at the polling
station of his constituency in Sedgefield . . .'

QUEEN ELIZABETH II, wearing formal robes of the Garter, is posing for an official portrait by an elderly black PORTRAIT ARTIST (representative, one assumes, of one of the many Charities of which she is patron) . . .

ELIZABETH
Have you voted yet, Mr Crawford?

ARTIST
(proudly dabbing palette)
Yes, Ma'am. I was there when they opened. First in line.
Seven o'clock.

TV COMMENTARY

'If he wins, he'll be the youngest Prime Minister in
almost two hundred years. All week he's been warning his
party against complacency but all the polls suggest the
result is now a foregone conclusion . . .'

He straightens . . .

ARTIST

And I don't mind telling you, it wasn't for Mr Blair.

ELIZABETH

Not a moderniser, then?

ARTIST

Certainly not. We're in danger of losing too much that's
good about this country as it is.

TV COMMENTARY

'The only questions that still remain: how big will his
landslide be? And how extensive, how sweeping will the
modernisation programme be that he ushers in?'

ELIZABETH

Hmm.

The QUEEN watches as he paints . . .

ELIZABETH *(cont'd.)*

I rather envy you being able to vote.
(a beat)
Not the actual ticking of the box, although, I suppose, it
would be nice to experience that ONCE.
(a beat)
But the sheer joy of being partial.

ARTIST

Yes . . .

The ARTIST squints as he scrutinises the canvas . . .

                    ARTIST
One forgets that as Sovereign, you are not entitled to
vote.

                  ELIZABETH
No.

                    ARTIST
Still, you won't catch me feeling sorry for you. You might
not be allowed to vote, Ma'am . . .
                    (a beat)
But it IS your Government.

                  ELIZABETH
Yes.

The QUEEN raises her eyebrow . . .

            ELIZABETH *(cont'd)*
I suppose that is some consolation.

                                    FADE TO BLACK

4. INT. BUCKINGHAM PALACE—
    QUEEN'S BEDROOM—DAY

*The QUEEN's face. Fast asleep. It's shortly before 8.00 am. Daylight filters
through the curtains. As does something else . . .*

The stirring sound of bagpipes . . .

5. EXT. BUCKINGHAM PALACE—
    INNER COURTYARD—DAY

The inner courtyard of Buckingham Palace. In a ritual unchanged since Queen Victoria, a uniformed PIPER, wearing a kilt of Ancient Hunting Stuart tartan, marches under her Majesty's windows, playing the bagpipes.

It's her morning alarm call, and it's the way she wakes up wherever she is—anywhere in the world.

6.   INT. BUCKINGHAM PALACE—
     QUEEN'S BEDROOM—DAY

Darkness. A soft knock at the door. (The strains of bagpipes can still be heard from below.) Her Majesty's DRESSER sticks her head round the corner, with a calling tray of Earl Grey tea and the newspapers.

DRESSER

G'morning, Ma'am.

The DRESSER puts the tea and newspapers on a bedside table.

DRESSER

Shall I draw the curtains?

The QUEEN's sleepy voice answers . . . 'Please.' The DRESSER goes to the window.

ELIZABETH (O.S.)

Did you stay up?

DRESSER

Yes, Ma'am.

ELIZABETH (O.S.)

And? Was it as expected . . . ?

The QUEEN's hand reaches for spectacles, then for the newspapers. She puts on her glasses.

DRESSER

Yes, Ma'am. Mr Blair, by a landslide.

The QUEEN's expression changes . . .

ELIZABETH

I see.

She lifts the newspaper up. The front page comes into sharp focus.

FULL FRAME: the beaming smile of TONY BLAIR, the new Prime Minister. The QUEEN stares back. Their eyes meet—as it were. Headlines tell us . . .

'IT'S BLAIR!', 'LANDSLIDE VICTORY FOR BLAIR'.

7.   INT. BUCKINGHAM PALACE—
     BREAKFAST ROOM—DAY

The QUEEN sits at breakfast. Reading the newspapers. Dogs under the table. A knock on the door, and ROBIN JANVRIN, (40's), her deputy Private Secretary, pops around . . .

JANVRIN

The Prime Minister is on his way, Ma'am.

ELIZABETH

To *BE*, Robin.
               (correcting, terse)
Prime Minister to *BE*.

The QUEEN frostily flicks a page, without looking up . . .

ELIZABETH *(cont'd)*

He hasn't asked my permission yet.

8. INT. BUCKINGHAM—CORRIDOR—DAY

The QUEEN and JANVRIN walk through a corridor of the Palace. It has the air of a grand hotel. Chintz. Flock. Long, gilded mirrors. Portraits on the walls . . .

ELIZABETH
He's a hard one to read, isn't he?

JANVRIN
Yes. On the one hand his background is quite establishment. Father a Conservative. A public school education at Fettes, where he was tutored by the same man as the Prince of Wales.

ELIZABETH
Well, we'll try not to hold that against him.

JANVRIN
On the other, his manifesto promises the most radical modernisation and shake-up of the Constitution in three hundred years.

ELIZABETH
Oh. Is he going to 'modernise' us, do you think?

JANVRIN
I wouldn't put it past him. He's married to a woman with known anti-Monarchist sympathies—you may remember her curtsey the first time you met. It could best be described as 'shallow'.

ELIZABETH
I don't measure the depth of a curtsey, Robin. I leave that to my sister.

JANVRIN
And I spoke to the Cabinet Secretary who said he was

expecting the atmosphere at Downing Street to be very informal. Everyone on first name terms.
> *(a beat)*

At the Prime Minister's insistence.

> ELIZABETH
> What? As in 'Call me Tony'?

> JANVRIN
> Yes.

The QUEEN's face puckers in distaste . . .

> ELIZABETH
> Oh. I'm not sure I like the sound of that.
> *(a beat)*
> Have we sent him a protocol sheet?

9.   EXT. MALL—DAY

ARCHIVE FOOTAGE: As TONY BLAIR'S motorcade drives down the Mall.

10.   EXT. BUCKINGHAM PALACE—DAY

The motorcade sweeps into the grand, inner quadrangle of Buckingham Palace, and stops at the King's door.

11.   INT. CAR—DAY

Three secret service BODYGUARDS leap out and open the car doors. TONY looks out at the Palace . . .

> TONY
> Funny, I'm actually rather nervous.

CHERIE

Why? You've met her often enough before.

TONY

I know. But never one to one. And never as Prime
Minister.

CHERIE

Remember, you're a man that's just been elected by the
whole country.

TONY

Yes. But she's still, y'know . . .

TONY looks up at the vast Palace in front of him . . .

TONY

The Queen.

12.   INT. BUCKINGHAM PALACE—
CORRIDOR/STAIRCASE—DAY

*A uniformed EQUERRY leads TONY and CHERIE through corridors, and
up a grand staircase . . .*

EQUERRY

When we reach the audience room, I will knock. We will
not wait to be called, we will go straight inside. Standing
by the door, we bow. From the neck. I will introduce you.
The Queen will extend her hand, you go to her, bow
again, then shake her hand.

TONY shoots his cuffs, 'Right', clears his throat.

EQUERRY *(cont'd)*

Couple of other things. It's 'Ma'am' as in ham, not
'Ma'am' as in farm.

TONY

Yes . . .

EQUERRY

And when you're in the Presence, at no point must you
show your back.

TONY

The 'Presence'?

EQUERRY

Yes, Sir. That's what it's called, when you're in her
Majesty's company.

*TONY turns, shoots a look at CHERIE, who sticks her fingers down her
throat. TONY smiles back . . .*

*The EQUERRY reaches a grand door, and knocks gently. Without waiting
for a reply, he enters . . .*

CHERIE is left in the corridor. Alone. She stares at a liveried FOOTMAN.

*He stares back. No life behind his eyes. CHERIE takes a seat on a chair. Eyes
widen to herself.*

13.   INT. BUCKINGHAM PALACE—
      AUDIENCE ROOM—DAY

*TONY and the EQUERRY enter, and gently bow their heads. The
EQUERRY then straightens, and announces . . .*

EQUERRY

Mr Blair, your Majesty.

*The QUEEN extends her hand. TONY walks forward, and shakes it. The
EQUERRY leaves. The door is then closed.*

ELIZABETH

Congratulations.

TONY

Thank you, Ma'am.

ELIZABETH

Your children must be very proud.

TONY

I hope so.

ELIZABETH

You've three, haven't you?

TONY

That's right.

ELIZABETH

How lovely. Such a blessing. Children.

The QUEEN and TONY take their seats . . .

ELIZABETH

So . . . Have we shown you how to start a nuclear war
yet?

TONY
(thrown)

No.

ELIZABETH

First thing we do, I believe.
(a beat)
Then we take your passport and spend the rest of the
time sending you around the world.

TONY

You obviously know my job better than I do.

ELIZABETH

Well, you *are* my tenth Prime Minister, Mr Blair. I'd like
to think there weren't too many surprises left. My first
was Winston Churchill. He sat in your chair, in frock
coat and top hat, and was kind enough to give a shy
young girl like me quite an education.

TONY

I can imagine.

ELIZABETH

With time, one has hopefully added experience to that
education, and a little wisdom—better enabling us to
execute our constitutional responsibility.
                    (a pointed addition)
To advise, guide and warn the government of the day.

TONY

Advice which I look forward to receiving.

ELIZABETH

Well, we will save that for our weekly meetings.
                    (a beat)
Now, if there's nothing else, I believe we have some
business to attend to . . .

TONY stares, then clicks . . .

TONY

Of course . . .

*He falls, rather extravagantly, on bended knee. The supplicant position of
deference . . .*

TONY *(cont'd)*

Your Majesty, the country has spoken . . . and I come now
to ask your permiss . . .

ELIZABETH
(interjecting)
No, no, no. It's usual for ME to ask the questions.

TONY winces. Wishes the ground would swallow him up.

ELIZABETH *(cont'd)*
Mr Blair, the people have elected you to be their leader.
And so the duty falls on me, as your Sovereign, to ask you
to become Prime Minister, and form a government in my
name.

TONY stares. Lost for words. Then . . .

ELIZABETH *(cont'd)*
Generally, this is where you say 'yes'.

TONY
'Yes'.

*The QUEEN extends her hand, which TONY kisses. She withdraws it
again—quite sharply, then DISCREETLY PRESSES A BUZZER by
her chair indicating the ceremony is over. The EQUERRY opens a door, and
CHERIE is invited inside.*

ELIZABETH
How nice to see you again, Mrs Blair.

CHERIE curtseys awkwardly, reluctantly, shallowly . . .

ELIZABETH *(cont'd)*
You must be very proud.

CHERIE

Yes.

ELIZABETH

And exhausted, I imagine. Where will you be spending
the summer?

CHERIE

France.

ELIZABETH

How lovely.

TONY

You'll be in Balmoral, I expect.

ELIZABETH

Yes, I can hardly wait. Wonderful place.

The QUEEN indicates a portrait of QUEEN VICTORIA . . .

ELIZABETH *(cont'd)*

My great, great grandmother said of it—'In Balmoral all
seems to breathe freedom and peace and to make one
forget the world and its sad turmoils.'

*At that moment, the doors open, and JANVRIN enters, and whispers urgently
in the QUEEN's ear. The QUEEN's face changes as she listens.*

ELIZABETH *(cont'd)*

Really . . . ?

Her expression changes. She frostily turns to the BLAIRS . . .

ELIZABETH *(cont'd)*

I'm afraid we're going to have to leave it there.

With that the QUEEN shakes TONY's hand. TONY and CHERIE awkwardly back out of the royal Presence, leaving the QUEEN and JANVRIN.

> ELIZABETH *(cont'd)*
> Not too short, was it? I gave him fifteen minutes.
> *(a beat)*
> One doesn't want to be rude.

14.   INT. BUCKINGHAM PALACE—CORRIDOR—DAY

TONY and CHERIE walk down a corridor. CHERIE whispers under her breath . . .

> CHERIE
> *(mimics QUEEN's manner)*
> 'Thank you so much for coming. Now bugger off.'

> TONY
> I know. What was all that about?

> CHERIE
> Diana. Apparently she's got a new boyfriend.

15.   ARCHIVE TELEVISION NEWS FOOTAGE

Of PRINCESS DIANA walking hand in hand with a dark-haired MAN in his late thirties . . .

> CNN NEWSREADER
> 'Dodi Al-Fayed is the son of Egyptian millionaire
> Mohammed Al-Fayed, a man whom the English
> establishment has repeatedly denied a British passport . . .'

16. TELEVISION NEWS FOOTAGE

DIANA and DODI kissing and canoodling on board the yacht Jonikal . . .

> GERMAN NEWSREADER
> 'The Princess and Mr Fayed were hugging and kissing in
> full view of the world's press yesterday . . .'

17. TELEVISION NEWS FOOTAGE

DIANA and DODI on the yacht on their last holiday together . . .

> FRENCH NEWSREADER
> '. . . the couple then left for Paris. At one point, the
> Princess told gathered reporters to watch out. Her next
> move would *really* surprise them . . .'

CUT TO:

18. EXT. RITZ HOTEL—NIGHT

PAPARAZZI are assembled outside the hotel. A few SPECTATORS too.

19. *CAPTION:* 'RITZ HOTEL, PARIS. 31 AUGUST, 1997'.

NEWS REPORTERS speak to camera outside the hotel . . .

> FRENCH REPORTER
> *(in French)*
> '. . . the Princess of Wales and Dodi Fayed returned to
> Paris earlier this afternoon.'

Beside the FRENCH REPORTER are other REPORTERS . . .

'. . . earlier today, they visited a local jewellery shop where unconfirmed reports suggested Mr Fayed had been looking at engagement rings . . .'

20.   INT. RITZ HOTEL—NIGHT

CCTV FOOTAGE: the unmistakable blonde hair of the PRINCESS of WALES as she enters the Ritz Hotel through revolving doors.

21.   EXT. RITZ HOTEL—NIGHT

A German REPORTER continues . . .

GERMAN REPORTER
(in German)
'. . . they have now been inside the hotel for more than two hours. We believe they have been dining in a suite on the fifth floor . . .'

Presently a ripple of activity: DOORMEN furtively speak into walkie-talkies. Growing anticipation in the CROWD . . .

An AMERICAN REPORTER turns to his camera . . .

AMERICAN REPORTER
'We've just been told the Princess is about to come out of the hotel . . .'

PAPARAZZI jostle roughly for position, and raise their cameras as the doors open, and a BLACK MERCEDES slides into position.

22.   INT. RITZ HOTEL—SAME TIME

Elsewhere in the hotel . . .

The real DIANA, her BODYGUARD, DODI FAYED, and HENRI PAUL leave the public part of the hotel, and walk down a flight of stairs . . .

23.   EXT. RITZ HOTEL—FRONT ENTRANCE—NIGHT

Pandemonium breaks out as BODYGUARDS emerge from the hotel. Engines of the decoy black Mercedes roar into life.

Doors slam. The CROWD surges. An explosion of flashbulbs. Tyres burn. The squeal of rubber as the MERCEDES pulls off.

Swarms of PAPARAZZI give chase, kick-starting their motorcycles, speaking into cell phones to their COLLEAGUES . . .

24.   INT. RITZ HOTEL—SAME TIME

The real ROYAL PARTY, meanwhile, walks briskly through an underground corridor which leads to the back door of the hotel . . .

25.   EXT. RITZ HOTEL—BACK EXIT—SAME TIME

PAPARAZZI who were waiting at the back exit, speak to their COLLEAGUES on their cell phones, and are about to jump on their motorcycles to join them in the chase, when suddenly . . .

HENRI PAUL, PRINCESS DIANA, her BODYGUARD and DODI FAYED emerge from a door, and climb into a waiting Mercedes. HENRI PAUL turns to the PAPARAZZI . . .

PAUL
(in French, we see subtitles)
Don't bother following. You won't catch us.

The engine starts with a roar. The PAPARAZZI double-take, and frantically shout into their phones to their COLLEAGUES. 'Wait! They've come out at the back.'

26.   EXT/INT. MERCEDES LIMOUSINE—NIGHT

The Mercedes pulls up at a traffic light.

ALL AROUND THEM: the glare of Paparazzi motorcycles and camera flashbulbs around the car. The Paparazzi call out in French and Italian. They thump the window. It's terrifying.

An explosion of flashing lights. Popping flashbulbs. The traffic light turns amber. DODI barks at the DRIVER . . .

The DRIVER, a short squat man in glasses (we do not see his face), slams his foot down.

27.   EXT. EXPRESSWAY—NIGHT

The car roars ahead, then speeds down into a tunnel, followed by the PAPA-RAZZI MOTORCYCLES.

FADE TO BLACK

28.   EXT. BALMORAL CASTLE—NIGHT

The Scottish Highlands. To establish.

The silhouette of a magnificent ten year old STAG stands on a rock, and roars into the night.

29. INT. CRAIGOWEN LODGE—NIGHT

'RRRRrrrinnnnggg', the phone rings . . .

A SILHOUETTE fumbles for a light switch, and hits the light. We immediately recognise the face. It's JANVRIN, the Queen's deputy Private Secretary.

> JANVRIN
> *(into phone)*
> Robin Janvrin.

He listens, then his expression changes.

> JANVRIN *(cont'd)*
> What?

He checks the clock on the bedside table, waking rapidly now. Deadly serious . . .

> JANVRIN *(cont'd)*
> Right. I see.

JANVRIN hangs up. Then urgently dials a number on the telephone . . .

30. INT. CRAIGOWEN LODGE—NIGHT

> JANVRIN *(cont'd)*
> I'm going to need to speak to her Majesty.
> *(a beat)*
> Right away.

31. EXT. BALMORAL ESTATE—NIGHT

Still pulling on clothes, JANVRIN rushes on foot towards the big house in the distance . . .

Lights go on all over the darkened castle.

32.   INT. BALMORAL—STAIRCASE. NIGHT

JANVRIN and a middle-aged DRESSER (half-asleep and still arranging her uniform), walk urgently up the stairs towards the second floor corridor where the QUEEN's bedroom is located. They pass a PAGE on the way down . . .

> JANVRIN *(cont'd)*
> Tell Sir Guy I'd like everyone in. As soon as possible.

The PAGE nods. Departs.

33.   INT. QUEEN'S BEDCHAMBER—NIGHT

A knock on the door. The door opens, and the DRESSER's voice gently calls out . . .

> DRESSER
> Ma'am?

The QUEEN stirs in her bed . . .

> DRESSER *(cont'd)*
> Mr. Janvrin is here to see you . . .

> ELIZABETH
> Oh . . .

The QUEEN turns on the light. The DUKE of EDINBURGH flinches in irritation, scrunching his eyes as they are blinded . . .

> PRINCE PHILIP
> What the . . . ?

34. INT. BALMORAL—CORRIDOR—NIGHT

The QUEEN emerges from her bedroom wearing an old-fashioned dressing-gown, and clutching a hottie (a velour-covered Cosimax hot water bottle), to find ROBIN JANVRIN waiting . . .

JANVRIN

Good evening, Ma'am. I'm sorry to disturb . . .

He clears his throat . . .

JANVRIN *(cont'd)*

I've just had a call from our Embassy in Paris. It's . . . the Princess of Wales.

PRINCE PHILIP appears in the doorway. Irritable.

PRINCE PHILIP

Why? What's she done now?

34A. INT. MYROBELLA—TRIMDON—TONY'S BEDROOM—NIGHT

'Rrrrrinng', the phone rings. We're in TONY BLAIR's constituency house in Trimdon, near Durham in northern England.

'Click', TONY, in T-shirt, turns on the light. His face is creased with sleep. He blinks . . .

TONY

Hello?

The figure of CHERIE stirs in the bed. Groans. TONY listens to the voice at the other end . . .

TONY *(cont'd)*

What? How badly?

Now he begins to wake. Sits up.

> TONY *(cont'd)*
> I see. Who are we speaking to there?

> TONY *(cont'd)*
> Right.
>> *(shell-shocked)*
> Keep me posted.

TONY hangs up. CHERIE turns . . .

> TONY *(cont'd)*
> It's Diana. She's been in a car accident. In Paris.

> CHERIE
> Is it serious?

> TONY
> Apparently Dodi Fayed is dead.

> CHERIE
> What?

CHERIE's face. Visibly shocked. TONY has switched on the TV in the bedroom.

> NEWSREADER
> 'Let's just re-cap on what's happened . . .'

35.   NO SCENE 35

36.   INT. BALMORAL—SITTING ROOM—NIGHT

The QUEEN is sitting with the DUKE OF EDINBURGH.

PRINCE PHILIP
What was she doing in Paris?

ELIZABETH
You know what she's like.

The QUEEN flicks channels, peering over her glasses, trying to catch the latest news on the television . . .

At that moment CHARLES enters the room. His face is ravaged with concern. It's the first time the QUEEN has seen him since news of the crisis . . .

ELIZABETH
It's quite awful . . .
(*wants to console CHARLES but finds it easier to say . . .)*
What are you going to do about the boys?

An awkward moment. Stifled . . .

CHARLES
Let them sleep until we know more.

ELIZABETH
Yes, that's sensible.

CHARLES
I should go to Paris. I told my people to start organising a
jet.

ELIZABETH
What? A *private* one?

CHARLES
Yes.

ELIZABETH
Isn't that precisely the sort of extravagance they attack us
for?

CHARLES

Well, how else am I going to get to Paris at this time of
night? The airport at Aberdeen will be closed.

Presently, a voice from behind . . .

QUEEN MOTHER

You can use the Royal Flight. They keep one of the
planes on permanent stand-by.
                    (deadpans)
In case I kick the bucket.

ELIZABETH

Out of the question. It's not a matter of State.

CHARLES

What are you talking about?

ELIZABETH

Diana is no longer an HRH, nor a member of the Royal
Family. This is a private matter.

CHARLES

She's mother to your grandchildren.

The QUEEN MOTHER sits on the sofa next to PRINCE PHILIP . . .

QUEEN MOTHER

What's the latest?

PRINCE PHILIP

I don't know. I can't hear . . .
                    (indicates TELEVISION)
Everyone's shouting!

CHARLES stares in disbelief. Exits the room . . .

37. INT. BALMORAL—JANVRIN'S OFFICE—NIGHT

A television plays in the corner . . .

> TELEVISION
> '. . . behind me, is the tunnel of the Pont de l'Alma,
> which you reach by the expressway along the Seine. It was
> along here that the Mercedes carrying the Princess . . .'

JANVRIN's SECRETARY hands over the phone . . .

> SECRETARY
> The Ambassador, in Paris.

> JANVRIN
> Good evening, Sir.

*JANVRIN listens to what the person is saying at the other end. His expression
changes . . .*

> JANVRIN *(cont'd)*
> Right.
> *(ashen-faced)*
> I see.

38. INT. BALMORAL—1ST FLOOR CORRIDOR—NIGHT

*An ashen-faced JANVRIN walks along the corridor, reaches the room where
the ROYAL FAMILY is watching television.*

He clears his throat, knocks on the door . . .

39. INT. BALMORAL—LARGE SITTING-ROOM—NIGHT

JANVRIN enters.

JANVRIN

I've just spoken to our Ambassador in Paris, Ma'am.

All heads turn to face him . . .

JANVRIN *(cont'd)*

I'm afraid it's not good news.

40.   INT. BALMORAL—CHARLES'S STUDY—
      SAME TIME (AYRSHIRE)

PRINCE CHARLES's face: he lets out a strangled cry, as he hears the news . . .

CHARLES *(cont'd)*

No!

CHARLES roars in pain and disbelief. His knuckles whiten . . .

CHARLES

No, no, no, no . . . !

In the doorway: STEPHEN LAMPORT, who has delivered the news, can hardly bear to watch . . .

41.   INT. BALMORAL—LARGE SITTING-ROOM—NIGHT

ON TV: struggling in vain to hold onto his composure, a BRITISH NEWS-READER relays the news, visibly in shock . . .

NEWSREADER

'We have just had confirmation, that Diana, Princess of
Wales . . .
                    (voice cracks)
. . . has died in Paris.'

ELIZABETH, PRINCE PHILIP and THE QUEEN MOTHER all stare. A tableau of shock.

A CNN ANCHOR breaks the news to a worldwide audience . . .

> CNN ANCHOR
> 'I'm afraid we have some bad news to report . . .'

41A.   INT. MYROBELLA—NIGHT

The CNN ANCHOR continues on TV.

> CNN ANCHOR *(cont'd)*
> 'Diana, Princess of Wales, is dead.'

TONY BLAIR is watching on TV, sitting downstairs, having thrown on some clothes. He speaks on the phone . . .

> TONY
> What have I got on this week?

41B.   INT. DOWNING STREET—SAME TIME

ALASTAIR CAMPBELL, Press Secretary to TONY BLAIR, is dressed and already in Downing Street. Also watching television. (WE INTERCUT BETWEEN THE TWO LOCATIONS AS NECESSARY.)

> ALASTAIR
> You're writing your maiden Conference speech as Prime Minister.

> TONY
> Well, let's cancel everything else. This is going to be massive.
> *(a beat)*
> I'd better make a statement in the morning.

ALASTAIR

You'll be pleased to know I've already started coming up
with ideas.

*On CAMPBELL's knee, a pad of paper. We pick out the words, 'People's
Princess.'*

TONY

God, she's only been dead an hour!

ALASTAIR

Would you prefer I *didn't* do my job?

42, 43.   NO SCENES 42 & 43

44.   INT. BALMORAL—CHILDREN'S CORRIDOR
      —NIGHT

*The QUEEN'S FACE in close-up. Her eyes flicker as she watches something
intently.*

*We REVERSE ANGLE to see: a half-open door. SILHOUETTES inside.
The sound of male voices. Whispering. Speaking softly.*

*It's the moment the BOYS are being told. We make out the SILHOUETTES
hugging. The sound of tears. Soft voices. CHARLES repeatedly kissing his
SONS.*

*Our CAMERA stays on the QUEEN's FACE. A distant flicker of pain at
the unrestrained intimacy and affection between them.*

Presently, the door opens, and a red-eyed PRINCE CHARLES emerges.

CHARLES

They're going to go back to sleep.
            (clears his throat, speaks with difficulty)
Well, try anyway.

The QUEEN goes up to CHARLES and stiffly, poignantly, tries to touch him. But cannot. Is unable. She withdraws her hand.

> CHARLES *(cont'd)*
> *(reading the message)*
> My Private Secretary's office has found a travel agency open in New York that will sell me a flight to Paris with an hour's stopover in Manchester.

CHARLES contains himself with difficulty . . .

> CHARLES *(cont'd)*
> Perhaps now you might consider whether it's still an extravagance to bring back the mother of the future King of England in one of our planes?

> ELIZABETH
> *(after a long pause)*
> All right.

CHARLES's eyes burn. He turns, and walks out.

The QUEEN is left alone. She stares for a moment, then leaves, passing a FOOTMAN.

> ELIZABETH *(cont'd)*
> *(to FOOTMAN)*
> I don't want the boys to see the news and get upset. First thing tomorrow morning, I want the radio taken out of their bedroom, and the television taken out of the nursery.

The FOOTMAN bows . . .

45.   INT. BALMORAL CASTLE—QUEEN'S BEDCHAMBER—VERY EARLY DAWN

The QUEEN sits in bed, writing her diary, in a bedchamber where the decor is unchanged in a hundred years . . .

Outside, the sound of bird-song. The first rays of light.

The DUKE OF EDINBURGH sticks his head around the corner. He looks at the QUEEN . . .

                    PRINCE PHILIP
Well, well, well.

                    ELIZABETH
Ye-es.

                    PRINCE PHILIP
Are you all right?

A silence.

                    PRINCE PHILIP *(cont'd)*
Your sister called about an hour ago.
From Tuscany.

                    ELIZABETH
I hope you told her to come back? Cut the holiday short?

                    PRINCE PHILIP
I did.

ELIZABETH raises her eyebrow . . .

                    ELIZABETH
Can't imagine she was pleased.

                    PRINCE PHILIP
That's putting it mildly.

ELIZABETH

What did she say?

PHILIP smiles to himself recalling MARGARET's words . . .

PRINCE PHILIP

Something about Diana managing to be even more
annoying dead than alive.

The QUEEN looks up . . .

ELIZABETH

Just make sure the boys never hear you talk like that.

PRINCE PHILIP

Fine. But deny you haven't thought the same.

*A silence. PHILIP produces a bottle of pills from his dressing-gown pocket,
and shakes them . . .*

PRINCE PHILIP *(cont'd)*

Something to help you go down?

ELIZABETH

No. I'm going to do my diary a little longer.

PRINCE PHILIP

Fine. I'll sleep next door.

*PHILIP touches her on the shoulder. But she doesn't reciprocate. He goes. The
QUEEN appears to continue writing, but our CAMERA slowly turns to re-
veal her PEN is not moving. Nor writing.*

She's staring in thought.

46.   EXT. MYROBELLA—DAY

A Victorian, red-brick house. In the driveway, the incongruous mix of a grey Renault Espace people-carrier and two POLICE VEHICLES.

In the modest garden: two ARMED POLICE OFFICERS are playing football with three young CHILDREN . . .

46A.   INT. TRIMDON—BLAIR KITCHEN—DAY

Inside the plain, unfashionably decorated house . . .

The TV plays in the corner of the kitchen. CHERIE BLAIR, visibly upset, watches TV while cooking breakfast.

TONY is not wearing his Newcastle shirt.

TONY is reading out his statement which is written on a pad of paper, filled with crossings-out . . .

> TONY
> '. . . that's how she will remain. In our minds, our hearts, forever.'
> *(looks up)*
> OK, got it.

46B.   INT. DOWNING STREET—SAME TIME.

ALASTAIR CAMPBELL is in Downing Street, sits in an office, feet on a desk, staring at the TV . . .

> ALASTAIR
> Where will you do it?

> TONY
> I thought at church. On the way in.

ON TV: breaking news: Diana's brother, EARL SPENCER, makes a statement from the gates outside his house in South Africa . . .

SPENCER (ON TV)

'. . . this is not a time for recriminations, however I would say that I always believed that the press would kill her in the end. But even I could not imagine that they would take such a direct hand in her death as seems to be the case. It would appear that every proprietor and editor of every publication that has paid for intrusive and exploitative photographs of her has blood on his hands today . . .'

ALASTAIR

Not the press, mate. You've got the wrong villain.

An AIDE appears in the doorway, catches TONY's eye, and indicates her watch . . .

TONY

I've got to go.

ALASTAIR

You about to speak to the Queen?

TONY

Yes.

ALASTAIR shoots a mischievous look . . .

ALASTAIR

Ask her if *SHE* greased the brakes.

TONY

Now, now . . .

TONY hangs up, crosses to the study, making sure the doors are shut so he won't be disturbed. We notice his shirt has no. 10 on the back, under the name, 'BLAIR'.

47, 48.   NO SCENES 47 & 48

49.   INT. BALMORAL—DINING ROOM—DAY

The QUEEN, PRINCE PHILIP and the QUEEN MOTHER sit in silence at the table, eating breakfast, stoically listening to radio coverage, soberly flicking through newspapers . . .

The QUEEN is the only one who is fully dressed (the others in bathrobes), and she wears black. She is reading the Sunday Times.

All around them the QUEEN's (elderly) MAIDS perform the choreography of service as the radio coverage continues. One MAID pours tea. Another brings fresh toast.

Also present is the rather smarter VALET and MAID belonging to the PRINCE of WALES, and his separate HOUSEHOLD. They have a separate (and more stylish) uniform of their own.

They set CHARLES's place and his breakfast (nuts, grains, healthy food). A flamboyant napkin is folded into an elaborate fleur-du-lis (traditional symbol of the PRINCE OF WALES). The QUEEN turns to Charles's VALET . . .

A knock on the door, JANVRIN enters, and bows in respect to the QUEEN . . .

JANVRIN

I'm sorry to disturb, Ma'am, but I've the Prime Minister, for you. From his constituency.

QUEEN MOTHER

(privately rolls eyes, without looking up from newspaper)
Lucky you.

· 34 ·

ELIZABETH

Thank you, Robin. I'll take it next door.

The QUEEN gets to her feet and walks out into . . .

50. INT. BALMORAL—FIRST FLOOR CORRIDOR—DAY

The first-floor corridor. STAFF flatten themselves against the wall, averting their eyes as . . .

The QUEEN unexpectedly comes out of the dining-room, walks along the corridor, and disappears into . . .

51. INT. BALMORAL—QUEEN'S STUDY—DAY

The QUEEN's study. High ceilings, portraits, stag's antlers on the wall. The QUEEN picks up the phone . . .

ELIZABETH *(cont'd)*

Good morning, Prime Minister.

52. INT. TRIMDON—BLAIR'S STUDY—DAY

The contrast in surroundings could hardly be greater. TONY sitting in a cramped room, surrounded by toys, in a track suit, in a working-class house . . .

TONY

Good morning, your Majesty. May I say right away how very sorry I am—and that the thoughts and prayers of my family are with you at this terrible time and with the two princes in particular.

ELIZABETH

Thank you.

CHERIE appears in the doorway.

> TONY
>
> Is it your intention to make some kind of appearance? Or statement?

> ELIZABETH
>
> Certainly not.

53.   INT. BALMORAL—QUEEN'S STUDY—DAY

The QUEEN's face, bristling at the suggestion. (WE INTERCUT AS NECESSARY) . . .

> ELIZABETH
>
> No member of the Royal family will speak publicly about this. It is a private matter and we would all appreciate it if it could be respected as such.

> TONY
>
> I see.

TONY straightens, taken aback . . .

> TONY *(cont'd)*
>
> I don't suppose anyone has had time to think about the funeral yet?

> ELIZABETH
>
> We've spoken to the Spencer family, and it's their wish . . .
> > *(a beat)*
> . . . their *express* wish, that it should be a private funeral. With a memorial service to follow in a month, or so.

> TONY
>
> Right.

TONY shoots a look at CHERIE . . .

> ELIZABETH
>
> Given that Diana was no longer a member of the Royal Family we have no choice but to respect their wishes.

> TONY
>
> I see.

TONY shoots a look at CHERIE . . .

> TONY *(cont'd)*
>
> You don't feel that in view of her high profile and popularity . . .
>> *(choosing his words carefully)*
>
> . . . it might be an idea to pay tribute to her life and achievements?
>> *(a beat)*
>
> Or even just to her as a mother?

The QUEEN's face freezes over.

> ELIZABETH
>
> As I said. That's the Spencers' wish.

> TONY
>
> And the public, Ma'am? The British People?

TONY hesitates . . .

> TONY *(cont'd)*
>
> You don't think a private funeral would be denying them a chance . . .

> ELIZABETH
>
> Chance to what . . . ?

TONY

To share in the grief?

The QUEEN's face: did she hear right?

ELIZABETH

It's a *family funeral*, Mr. Blair. Not a fairground attraction.
(*a beat*)
I think the Princess has already paid a high enough price
for exposure to the press, don't you?

*PRINCE PHILIP enters, dressed and ready for church. He indicates his
watch . . .*

ELIZABETH (*cont'd*)

Now, if there is nothing else I must get on. The children
have to be looked after.

TONY

Of course.

'Click', the QUEEN hangs up. TONY stares at the receiver.

TONY (*cont'd*)

Good-bye, Your Majesty.

He puts down the phone . . .

TONY (*cont'd*)

Her instinct is to do nothing. Say nothing. And give her a
private funeral.

CHERIE

Are you surprised? She hated her guts.

TONY

Well, I think it's a mistake.

TONY's face becomes dark . . .

>   TONY *(cont'd)*
> They screwed up her life. Let's hope they don't screw up
> her death.

54.   INT. SALOON/HALL—BALMORAL—DAY

*Everyone is getting ready to go to church. The QUEEN and QUEEN
MOTHER are putting on their hats. PRINCE PHILIP, in full Highland
regalia and black tie, helps both LADIES into their long coats . . .*

>   ELIZABETH
> The Chaplain called. Wanted to know whether he should
> make any changes to the service or make special mention
> of Diana.

>   PRINCE PHILIP
> What did you say?

>   ELIZABETH
> I told him he shouldn't change a thing.

>   QUEEN MOTHER
> Quite right.

>   ELIZABETH
> I think the less fuss one makes, or draws attention to it,
> the better.
> *(she lowers her voice, as the PRINCES approach from the saloon with
> CHARLES)*
> For the boys.

>   QUEEN MOTHER
> Yes.

ELIZABETH

And we should probably arrange some company for
them. Some young people.

PRINCE PHILIP

I'll take them for a long walk this afternoon. Up Craggy
Head.

ELIZABETH

Good. They'd like that.

PRINCE PHILIP opens the doors . . .

ELIZABETH *(cont'd)*

But no guns. It's Sunday.

They walk off to the waiting CARS . . .

55. INT. DOWNING STREET—SAME TIME

*Offices BUSY FOR SUNDAY. Bustling AIDES and SECRETARIES. The
engine room of Government. An AIDE sticks his head round a door, and calls
down the corridor to . . .*

AIDE

Alastair? He's on . . .

*CAMPBELL turns, and excuses himself from his conversation, walks back
down the corridor . . .*

56. INT. OFFICE—DAY

*ALASTAIR enters a press 'monitoring' room, where several televisions are
playing. One or two AIDES are busy working . . .*

ON TV: TONY, wearing a dark suit, and tie, takes his position in front of the statue of the Virgin Mary, in front of the cameras.

57.   EXT. TRIMDON CHURCH—DAY

TONY steps closer to the microphones, then . . .

> TONY
>
> We are today a nation in a state of shock, in mourning, in grief that is so deeply painful to us. People everywhere, not just here in Britain, kept faith with Princess Diana . . .

58.   INT. BALMORAL CASTLE—DAY

JANVRIN watches the broadcast on television, surrounded by several MEMBERS OF STAFF—MAIDS, COOKS, VALETS, FOOTMEN, all craning their necks, watching the television in the Private Secretary's room . . .

Our camera stays on JANVRIN's face, as TONY's speech continues . . .

> TONY (ON TV) *(cont'd)*
> 'They liked her, they loved her, they regarded her as one of the People. She was the People's Princess, and that is how she will stay, how she will remain in our hearts and memories forever . . .'

JANVRIN's eyes roll privately . . .

> JANVRIN
> A bit over the top, don't you think?

JANVRIN turns, fully expecting everyone to agree . . .

But instead all the STAFF MEMBERS behind him have tears rolling down their cheeks . . .

59.   EXT. HOSPITAL—PARIS—DAY

Archive Footage.

CHARLES's motorcade pulls up outside the hospital in Paris. Doors open. PRINCE CHARLES gets out . . .

60.   INT. HOSPITAL—CORRIDOR—PARIS—DAY

Shooting through the half-open door: we watch as the PRINCE of WALES disappears into the room. In the far corner, an open coffin.

CHARLES is visibly distressed. We hear the PRIEST's voice as he begins to pray . . .

PRIEST
Nôtre Père qui es aux cieux,
Que ton nom soit sanctifié,
Que ton règne vienne,
Que ta volonté soit faite,
Sur la terre comme au ciel . . .

In the corridor: hospital OFFICIALS quietly close the door in respect.

61.   TELEVISION NEWS FOOTAGE

PRESIDENT BILL CLINTON, fighting emotion, speaking from the White House lawn . . .

CLINTON (ON TV)
'I'll always be glad I knew the Princess, and hope
everyone will support her two fine sons and help them
have the life and the future she would want . . .'

PRESIDENT NELSON MANDELA—speaking from Cape Town . . .

MANDELA (ON TV)
'I had the honour of hosting her a few months ago when
she visited our country, and I was tremendously impressed
by her . . .'

The sound of a NEWSREADER's voice . . .

NEWSREADER (V.O.)
'In cities all around the world, shrines have been created,
in a spontaneous, worldwide outpouring of grief.'

*Images of NEW YORKERS laying flowers outside the British Embassy,
AUSTRALIANS doing the same in Sydney, PAKISTANIS in Karachi . . .*

62.   INT. CAR—DAY

*TONY BLAIR is in a car on his way back down to London. The phone rings.
He is travelling with an AIDE, who answers the phone, listens, then hands it
to TONY . . .*

AIDE
Lord Airlie.

TONY shoots a look, 'Who?' The AIDE covers the phone . . .

AIDE *(cont'd)*
The Lord Chamberlain. In charge of the funeral. You're
meeting him at the airport.

TONY nods. Takes the phone.

TONY

Lord Airlie.

63.   INT. CAR—SAME TIME

A rather formidable, handsome, aristocratic man with a military bearing, is driven in a car, speaking into a mobile phone . . .

LORD AIRLIE
(brisk, military)
Prime Minister. I'm responsible for organising all royal ceremonial events . . .
(a beat)
And there's simply no precedent for the funeral of an ex-HRH.

64.   INT. CAR—SAME TIME

TONY privately rolls his eyes at the ridiculous upper-class pronunciation . . .

TONY
Then perhaps we should plan for any contingency.

LORD AIRLIE
Yes. I've arranged a meeting tomorrow morning at 10.00 at Buckingham Palace. Officials from all three palaces, representatives from the Spencer Family, the emergency services.
(a beat)
Would you send some of your people?

TONY
Absolutely. Of course.

They hang up.

TONY *(cont'd)*
(mimicking posh accent)
'Preeecedent?'

TONY stares . . .

TONY *(cont'd)*
Where do they *find* these people?

65.   EXT. RAF NORTHOLT—DAY

PRINCE CHARLES comes down the steps of his plane. He walks towards the line of OFFICIALS, among them TONY BLAIR who stands next to LORD AIRLIE. TONY and PRINCE CHARLES shake hands . . .

TONY
I'm so sorry, Sir. And if there's anything I or my Government can do . . .

CHARLES appears distracted. Miles away . . .

CHARLES
They stood up as we drove past . . . in cafes . . . in restaurants. Removed their hats. This was Paris. One of the busiest cities in the world . . . and you could hear a pin drop . . .

TONY
I imagine it will be the same here.

CHARLES
Yes . . . I imagine it will.

CHARLES looks at TONY . . .

CHARLES *(cont'd)*
The Palace would still prefer to see it as a private funeral.
What are your feelings on that?

TONY
I . . .
(a diplomatic smile)
I think that would present us with difficulties.

CHARLES
So do I. My mother . . .
(corrects himself)
. . . the Queen, comes from a generation not best
equipped to . . .
(tailing off)
. . . she grew up in the war . . .
(a beat)
I think what we need, what the COUNTRY needs is to
be led by someone . . . 'of today'. If you follow?
(a beat)
Balmoral is . . .
(he gestures, 'another world')

TONY
I think I understand.

CHARLES and TONY shake hands, then the PRINCE moves on . . .

Meanwhile, in the background, DIANA's coffin is taken from the aeroplane by pall-bearers and loaded into a hearse.

The coffin is draped in the ROYAL STANDARD . . .

66.   INT. BALMORAL—LARGE SITTING-ROOM—NIGHT

The QUEEN, PRINCE PHILIP and the QUEEN MOTHER watch television. It's the evening news . . .

ON TV: PRINCE CHARLES is greeted by PRESIDENT CHIRAC on the steps of the hospital.

ELIZABETH
Have we heard from the Spencers again? Have they made up their minds when the funeral will be?

QUEEN MOTHER
Not me. No one tells me anything.

NEWSREADER (V.O.)
'The Prince of Wales spent half an hour at the hospital. At 5.06, the party left with Diana's coffin . . .'

PRINCE PHILIP
On our walk today, one of the ghillies said he'd seen a large stag up at Craghie Head.
(a beat)
He reckoned fourteen points.

QUEEN MOTHER
What? Really? We haven't had one that big on this estate in years.

PRINCE PHILIP
No. Quite.

ON TV: CHARLES's plane arrives back in England.

NEWSREADER (V.O.)
'Diana's coffin arrived back in London, at RAF Northolt, two hours later . . .'

The QUEEN watches intently as CHARLES is greeted on the runway by TONY BLAIR, and the two men talk.

A flicker of suspicion on the QUEEN's face . . .

PRINCE PHILIP

Anyway, I thought it might be a good distraction. For the
boys.

ELIZABETH

What? Stalking?

The QUEEN looks up . . .

ELIZABETH *(cont'd)*

Isn't it a bit soon?

PRINCE PHILIP

I think anything that gets them outside is a good idea.

NEWSREADER (V.O.)

'Earlier today, the Prime Minister made a statement from
his constituency . . .'

*ON TV: TONY making his speech outside the church in Trimdon. We
CLOSE on the QUEEN's face as she hears . . .*

TONY (ON TV)

'They liked her. They loved her. They regarded her as one
of the People. She was the People's Princess, and that is
how she will remain in our hearts forever . . .'

The QUEEN watches in disbelief. Her knuckles whiten.

ELIZABETH

I'm sorry, I can't bear it.
                    (gets to her feet)
I'm going to bed.

The QUEEN walks out.

67.   EXT. BUCKINGHAM PALACE—DAY

The following morning. A bare flagpole. No flag flying.

But the flowers left by mourners outside the Palace gates are growing.

68.   INT. BUCKINGHAM PALACE—MEETING ROOM—DAY

A large ceremonial room. Elaborate chinoiserie. Ming vases. Inside, some thirty or forty OFFICIALS, many uniformed, sit around a table. Among them: the CHIEF CONSTABLE of the METROPOLITAN police, the heads of the FIRE SERVICE and AMBULANCE SERVICE, military OFFICERS, representatives from the three palaces, Kensington Palace (DIANA's court), St James's Palace (CHARLES's court), and Buckingham Palace (the QUEEN's court), representatives from the Intelligence and Police Protection services, experts in protocol, and finally, representatives from the SPENCER FAMILY and Downing Street (among them ALASTAIR CAMPBELL).

LORD AIRLIE (whom we met at RAF Northolt) checks the time. It's ten o'clock. He raps on a table, calling the meeting to order . . .

> LORD AIRLIE
> Right. It's ten o'clock. Let's make a start.

> LORD AIRLIE *(cont'd)*
> Thank you all for coming at such notice. I think we all agree this is an extraordinarily sensitive occasion which presents us with tremendous challenges logistically . . .

> LORD AIRLIE *(cont'd)*
> *(a beat)*
> . . . constitutionally . . .
> *(a beat)*
> . . . practically . . .
> *(a beat)*
> . . . diplomatically . . .
> *(a beat)*
> . . . procedurally . . .

ALASTAIR privately rolls his eyes . . .

ALASTAIR

Oh, Christ . . .

69. EXT. DOWNING STREET—DAY

10, Downing Street. A car pulls up. ALASTAIR CAMPBELL gets out. Visibly in a bad mood.

70. INT. DOWNING STREET—DAY

TONY BLAIR is in his office, surrounded by his AIDES, working in shirtsleeves.

TONY

. . . after eighteen years of Opposition, of frustration and despair, I am proud, privileged, to stand before you as the new Prime Minister . . .

AIDE

Labour Prime Minister . . .

TONY

I want to set an ambitious course to modernise this country. To breathe new life into our institutions. To make privilege something for the many, not the few. So that we become nothing less than a beacon to the world . . .

'Thump', the door opens, ALASTAIR CAMPBELL enters, clutching the day's newspapers . . .

ALASTAIR

Bloody hell! You think the Royals are nutters! You should
meet their flunkeys! Two and a half hours on whether she
should be carried in a hearse or a gun-carriage.
(taps head, 'Nuts')
Anyway, raves in the press.

ALASTAIR *dumps the papers on the desk* . . .

ALASTAIR *(cont'd)*

This lot call you 'The Nation's Mourner in Chief', this lot
say you're 'The only person who has correctly judged the
mood of the country'. Even the *Mail* . . .
(disdainfully holding the paper between finger and thumb)
. . . was impressed.

ALASTAIR *drops the papers on TONY's desk.*

ALASTAIR *(cont'd)*

'People's Princess', mate. You owe me.

ALASTAIR *goes. TONY watches, then jumps up, opens the door. His AIDE
calls after him, covering the phone* . . .

AIDE

Gordon for you.

TONY

Tell him to hang on.

70A.   INT. DOWNING STREET—CORRIDOR—DAY

TONY *follows ALASTAIR out, calls after him* . . .

TONY *(cont'd)*

So it's decided? It's going to be a public funeral.

ALASTAIR

Yes. On Saturday. A whopper. The Abbey. The works.

TONY

Good. Has anyone told the Queen yet?

ALASTAIR

Dunno. No doubt some flunkey will be despatched.
Grovelling on all fours.

TONY smiles imagining the prospect, goes back into his office.

71. INT. BALMORAL CASTLE—
     LARGE SITTING-ROOM—DAY

*'Knock', a knock on the door, and ROBIN JANVRIN enters carrying a large
file. He bows first to the QUEEN . . .*

JANVRIN

Good morning, Ma'am.

. . . then to the QUEEN MOTHER . . .

JANVRIN *(cont'd)*

. . . Ma'am.

The QUEEN looks up . . .

ELIZABETH

What can we do for you, Robin?

JANVRIN braces himself. This is not going to be easy . . .

JANVRIN

Ma'am, there was a meeting at the Palace this morning.

ELIZABETH

About the funeral arrangements, yes.

JANVRIN

The Lord Chamberlain faxed over these plans for you to
consider.

JANVRIN puts a large file on her desk . . .

JANVRIN *(cont'd)*

There is now general agreement, Ma'am, that a public
funeral would be more appropriate.

ELIZABETH

I see.

The QUEEN perceptibly bristles . . .

ELIZABETH *(cont'd)*

And what form will it take?

JANVRIN

At the moment, they're suggesting . . .
(clears throat)
And of course these are early days . . .

*JANVRIN braces himself. Shoots a nervous look at the QUEEN
MOTHER . . .*

JANVRIN *(cont'd)*

. . . basing it on Tay Bridge.

The QUEEN MOTHER looks up. Horrified.

QUEEN MOTHER

Tay *Bridge* . . . ?

ELIZABETH

What . . . ?

A stunned silence . . .

QUEEN MOTHER

B-but that's the code name for *my* funeral?

JANVRIN

Indeed, Ma'am.
(a beat)
But it would be for practical reasons only.

JANVRIN is dying.

JANVRIN *(cont'd)*

It's the only one which has been . . .
(treads delicately)
. . . 'rehearsed'. The only one that could be put together . . . in time.

The QUEEN MOTHER needs to sit down . . .

QUEEN MOTHER

But I supervised those plans myself.

JANVRIN

Indeed, and the Lord Chamberlain was at pains to stress the *spirit* of the occasion will be quite different.
(a beat)
For example, in place of four hundred soldiers marching behind the coffin, the suggestion is that four hundred representatives from the Princess's various charities march behind the coffin.

ELIZABETH

I see . . .

The QUEEN MOTHER's eyes widen . . .

JANVRIN
And that instead of foreign Heads of State and Crown
heads of Europe, the guests would include a sprinkling of
actors of stage and screen, fashion designers and
other . . .
> (clears throat)

. . . celebrities . . .

QUEEN MOTHER

Celebrities . . . ?

ELIZABETH

Oh.

*The QUEEN looks ashen. The QUEEN MOTHER is pouring herself a
drink . . .*

ELIZABETH *(cont'd)*

Wa . . . was there anything else?

JANVRIN

No, Ma'am.

JANVRIN bows, and leaves. Then stops, remembering . . .

JANVRIN *(cont'd)*

Oh, yes. One other thing. The Police Commissioner was
keen that you consider the idea of a condolence book.
> (a beat)

It would give the growing crowds something to do. Make
marshalling them easier.

ELIZABETH
(distracted)

Yes, of course . . .

JANVRIN reaches the door . . .

                    JANVRIN
    Oh, and the flowers.

The QUEEN looks up . . .

                    ELIZABETH
    What flowers?

                    JANVRIN
    The flowers that have been left outside Buckingham
    palace. Currently they're blocking the path through the
    main gate, and will make things difficult for the
    Changing of the Guard.

                    ELIZABETH
    Fine. Then move them away.

JANVRIN flinches slightly in anticipation . . .

                    JANVRIN
    Actually, the Lord Chamberlain was wondering whether
    we shouldn't *leave* the flowers, and send the Guards
    through the North Gate.

The QUEEN looks thrown . . .

                    ELIZABETH
    Ye-es. Of course.
                        (chastened)
    Quite right.

71A.   INT. TONY'S OFFICE—DAY

'Rrrrinng', the phone rings. TONY is sitting at his desk with one AIDE. A
knock on the door. Another AIDE enters . . .

Stephen Lamport on one.

TONY looks up. Irritated at being disturbed . . .

TONY

Who?

AIDE

The Prince of Wales's private secretary. In Balmoral.
                    (covering phone)
He said it was urgent.

TONY rolls his eyes, then picks up the phone.

TONY

Good afternoon.

LAMPORT (v.o.)

Good afternoon, Prime Minister.

72.   NO SCENE 72

73.   INT. BALMORAL—CHARLES'S STUDY—DAY

*STEPHEN LAMPORT, Private Secretary to the Prince of Wales, sits at a
desk. CHARLES is also present, listening . . .*

LAMPORT

The Prince of Wales wanted me to thank you again for
your kind words yesterday.

TONY

Not at all.

He feels you and he . . . are modern men . . . of similar
mind . . .
>   *(a beat)*

. . . who could work well together at this difficult time.

TONY shoots a quizzical look . . .

TONY

Well, please thank his Highness, and assure him that he
can count on my full support. At all times.
>   *(a beat)*

Was that it?

LAMPORT

Yes.

TONY hangs up. He turns to his AIDE . . .

TONY

Bizarre. Why is Charles doing this?

AIDE

What?

TONY

Creeping up to me like this. He did it at the airport when
he asked me to 'deal' with his mother.

AIDE #2

Because he knows that if the Queen continues to get it
wrong over Diana, it won't be long before the Royals
become public enemy no 1.
>   *(a beat)*

Terrified of being shot, apparently.

TONY

Who, Charles?

AIDE

His people have already been onto us asking for extra
protection.

AIDE #2

He probably thinks if he's seen to be on our side, the
Queen will be the one left in the firing line, not him.

TONY

What? So it's OK for his *mother* to take the bullet, not
him?
                    (shakes head)
What a family.

AIDE

Can't stand one another apparently.

TONY

Who? Charles and the Queen? Yes, I heard that.
                    (a beat)
I suppose he won't be King until she dies, and she'll live
to 500.

TONY *(cont'd)*

They all do. Can't be much fun for her, either. Having her
natural successor breathing down her neck. Thinking
murderous thoughts. The whole thing . . .
                    (a beat)
It's like "The Agamemnon."

74.   EXT. BALMORAL CASTLE—COURTYARD—DAY

The QUEEN, in tatty old Barbour, head-scarf, Wellington boots, loads Cor-
gis and picnic hampers into the back of an old Land Rover. She climbs into the
old, muddy jeep, and starts the oily, smoky diesel engine. As she begins to drive
out, she turns a corner, and passes CHARLES who is climbing into his much
smarter, luxury, leather-upholstered jeep . . .

CHARLES

Wait! Where are they?

ELIZABETH

Up at Craigghead.

CHARLES

I'll come with you.

CHARLES climbs in. The QUEEN notices how extravagantly dressed he is. A kilt and tailored hunting jacket . . .

CHARLES *(cont'd)*

Want me to drive?

ELIZABETH

Certainly not.

CHARLES shudders at the rough interior of the car, the mud-spattered windows, the hard, uncomfortable ride . . .

CHARLES

I thought you were going to get a new one of these?

ELIZABETH

What for? It's perfectly all right.

The engine splutters as she changes gear. The car lurches forward.

75.   INT/EXT. JEEP—BALMORAL ESTATE—DAY

The QUEEN drives hard through woods, dust kicking up in the old Land Rover's wake. It's a bone-shaking ride.

CHARLES stares out of the window, lost in thought . . .

CHARLES

I was thinking last night what Diana might have done
had it been me that died in the tunnel in Paris.

The QUEEN privately rolls her eyes . . .

CHARLES *(cont'd)*

She would certainly have taken the boys to Paris. I rather
regret not doing that now.

ELIZABETH

What? And expose them to the media? It would have
been a dreadful thing to do. They're much better off here.

CHARLES

Look, whatever else you may have thought of Diana—
she was a *wonderful* mother.
(a beat)
She *adored* those boys. And never let them forget it.
(a beat)
Always warm.

The QUEEN's hands tighten on the steering wheel . . .

CHARLES *(cont'd)*

And physical.
(a beat)
Never afraid to show her feelings.

ELIZABETH

Especially whenever a photographer was in sight.

CHARLES

Yes, she MAY have encouraged all that, but still . . .

CHARLES looks out of the window. His eyes mist over . . .

CHARLES *(cont'd)*

That was always the extraordinary thing about her. Her
weaknesses and transgressions only seemed to make the
public love her MORE. Yet ours only make them hate us.
Why is that?

CHARLES looks up . . .

CHARLES *(cont'd)*

Why do they hate us so much?

The QUEEN mutters under her breath . . .

ELIZABETH

Not 'us', dear.

CHARLES
(not having heard)

What?

*The QUEEN salutes GAME-KEEPERS who remove their hats as the
QUEEN roars past.*

CHARLES *(cont'd)*

Yesterday, when we drove the coffin back into London,
there was a noise. A bang. I don't mind telling you I
thought it was a gun.

CHARLES's hands wring in anxiety . . .

CHARLES *(cont'd)*

I thought someone had taken a shot at me.

*The QUEEN hits the brakes, and pulls up. Visibly irritated by her son's
weakness. She opens the door, and steps out . . .*

ELIZABETH

Why don't you go on without me? I'm going to walk
back . . .

CHARLES

Are you sure?

ELIZABETH

Yes. It looks like rain . . .
                    (the DOGS jump out)
And I'm not in the mood for stalking anyway.

CHARLES knows better than to contradict his mother. He gets into the driving seat, puts on the safety belt, and drives off.

The Land Rover disappears in a cloud of dust.

The QUEEN straightens, then notices her shoe-laces are undone. The DOGS bark excitedly.

ELIZABETH *(cont'd)*

Wait! My shoe-lace is undone. You don't want me to trip
and hurt myself, do you?
                    (a beat)
You wouldn't get any proper walks then.

The QUEEN blissfully chatters away to the DOGS. So much easier than people . . .

ELIZABETH *(cont'd)*

Right. Done. Now who knows the way home?

The DOGS yap excitedly, immediately scamper off in the direction of the castle . . .

ELIZABETH *(cont'd)*

You clever things!

76.   EXT. SCOTTISH HIGHLANDS—DAY

CHARLES's Land Rover drives up into the hills, into spectacular landscape. A mile or two ahead, above the tree-line, PHILIP, the two PRINCES and STALKERS carrying guns, crawl on their bellies in pursuit of their quarry . . .

A hundred yards ahead of them, the STAG, unaware of the danger, imperiously, grazes on the grass . . .

DISSOLVE TO:

77.   INT. BALMORAL CASTLE—
      QUEEN'S BEDCHAMBER—NIGHT

The QUEEN, granite-faced, still smarting from her row with CHARLES, is in her bedroom. A nightcap martini is on her bedside table. She is writing her diary.

PHILIP emerges from the bathroom, appears in the doorway . . .

ELIZABETH
I spoke to Charles this afternoon.

A flicker of coldness behind her eyes . . .

ELIZABETH *(cont'd)*
Who was good enough to share with me his views on motherhood.

PRINCE PHILIP
What did he say?

A TV plays in the corner. DIANA, starved thin, panda-eyes, the infamous Martin Bashir 'PANORAMA' interview . . .

ELIZABETH

How *wonderful* Diana was.

PRINCE PHILIP

That's changing his tune.

ELIZABETH

What a natural.

DIANA (ON TV)

'. . . I think . . . they see me as a threat of some kind . . .'

PRINCE PHILIP sees what's on television, then grimaces . . .

PRINCE PHILIP
(puckers face)

Oh, for God's sake . . .

ELIZABETH

Maybe he's got a point. Maybe we are partly to blame.

PHILIP goes over to the television . . .

PRINCE PHILIP

I can't watch this.

ELIZABETH

No, wait. Leave it.

PHILIP stares at the screen . . .

DIANA (ON TV)

'Every strong woman in history has had to walk down a similar path . . .'

ELIZABETH

We encouraged the match. And signed off on it. Both of us.

                              (a beat)
You were very enthusiastic, remember.

                         PRINCE PHILIP
She was a nice girl. Then.

                         DIANA (ON TV)
'And I think it's this strength that causes the confusion
and the fear.'

PRINCE PHILIP shakes his head . . .

                         PRINCE PHILIP
And I was sure he'd give the other one up. Or, at least
make sure his wife toed the line.
                           (a gesture)
Isn't that what everyone does?

A flicker behind the QUEEN's eyes.

                           ELIZABETH
Is it?

*Her knuckles momentarily whiten. Unaware, PHILIP stares at the televi-
sion . . .*

                         DIANA (ON TV)
'Why is she strong? Where is she getting it from? Where
is she going to take it? How is she going to use it?'

He rolls his eyes in disbelief . . .

                         PRINCE PHILIP
I can't bear it any more. If you're watching, I'll sleep in
here. Early start tomorrow . . .
                      (kisses her on the forehead)
See you in the morning.

PHILIP goes, leaving the QUEEN staring. Still stinging from his remark about adultery.

'ZAP', she angrily hits the remote. The picture goes black.

78.   INT. DOWNING STREET—BLAIR'S HOME—NIGHT

TONY BLAIR and CHERIE at home, watching television. It's 10 o'clock. The KIDS are in bed, but their TOYS are still strewn around the sitting-room. TONY is tidying them up into boxes . . .

ON SCREEN: British historian DAVID STARKEY is lambasting CHARLES. TONY and CHERIE sit on the sofa, watching television, eating pasta on their knees. STARKEY defends the QUEEN. Part of an older generation. She knows no better.

CHERIE

How much of all this could be the first stirrings of . . .

TONY

What?

CHERIE

. . . I don't know . . . something more interesting. Maybe this time people have finally seen them for what they are.

TONY

Which is?

CHERIE

A bunch of freeloading, emotionally retarded . . . nutters.

TONY
(rolls eyes)

That's just absurd.

CHERIE

Why? They exist in a ludicrous cocoon of privilege and
wealth. They don't pay tax.

TONY

Yes, they do.

CHERIE

The Queen alone costs us what? Thirty, forty million a
year . . .

TONY reaches the door, and turns . . .

TONY

Not you, too. Look . . . if you want to have a serious
conversation about this . . .

CHERIE

I do . . .

TONY

. . . about the Constitution . . .

CHERIE

We don't HAVE one . . .

TONY

. . . or about ways in which we as a Government could
begin to phase out hereditary privileges, then fine.

CHERIE
(indicating plates)
If you're going, take the dishes . . .

TONY comes back to take the dirty plates . . .

TONY

But spare me the whole . . . 'off with their heads' thing.

CHERIE

Why?

TONY

Because it insults your intelligence.

CHERIE

'The case for reform is simple and obvious. It is in
principle wrong and absurd that people should wield
power on the basis of birth, not merit or election.'
(a beat)
YOUR words, not mine.

TONY is momentarily thrown . . .

TONY

Well, maybe now I've grown up.
(a beat)
It's *unimaginable* this country being a republic. Certainly
in *her* lifetime.

CHERIE

Why?

TONY

Because . . . no would would wear it.
(can't help laughing at the idea)
No one WANTS it.
(gestures)
It's just . . . daft.

TONY heads for the door . . .

CHERIE

It's not a mother thing, is it?

TONY turns . . .

CHERIE *(cont'd)*

Think about it. If she were still alive, wouldn't Hazel be exactly the same age? Whenever you talk about your mother, you mention her stoicism. Her frugality. Her sense of duty. The fact she was brought up in the way. Well c'mon . . . ?
(a beat)
Who does THAT sound like?

TONY smiles.

TONY

I'm going to do the washing-up.

FADE TO BLACK

78A.   INT. DOWNING STREET—CORRIDOR—DAY

ALASTAIR and TONY walk through the labyrinthine corridors and busy offices . . .

ALASTAIR

All right, the good news is that the Palace has agreed to video screens in the Royal Parks.

TONY

And the bad news?

ALASTAIR

Crash barriers.

TONY

What about them?

ALASTAIR

They're now predicting more than two million people will descend on London, and there aren't enough barriers to line the route. So we've gone cap in hand to the French for theirs. And there's something else I think you should see.

ALASTAIR leads TONY into . . .

79. NO SCENE 79

80. INT. DOWNING STREET—
    MONITORING ROOM—DAY

TONY follows ALASTAIR into an office where a television plays in the corner. Several young AIDES and INTERNS are watching, recording, making notes. Shirtsleeves, feet on desks. Informal.

> ALASTAIR
> Can we run that piece again? You're going to love this.

An INTERN puts in a video, hits the 'play' button. ON SCREEN: several members of the public complain about the royals. TONY watches for a moment, then . . .

> TONY
> Look, I know all this . . .

> ALASTAIR
> There!

One member of the public complains about the flag . . .

> TONY
> Don't tell me. There isn't a flag flying at half-mast above Buckingham Palace.

TONY rolls his eyes to himself.

TONY *(cont'd)*

God. Will someone save these people from
themselves . . .
                (irritated)
Fine. I'll call Balmoral . . .

TONY turns away, walks towards the door.

ALASTAIR

'Planet Zog'?

TONY

Because as Prime Minister of this country, I've really got
nothing better to do . . .

TONY walks out . . .

81.   NO SCENE 81

82.   EXT. BALMORAL ESTATE—DAY

*The ROYAL FAMILY is gathered for a barbecue lunch. At a distance, the
BOYS are in the river, being taught fishing by a GHILLIE . . .*

*PRINCE PHILIP stands by a barbecue, struggling to get the fire to light.
The QUEEN MOTHER is in another corner . . .*

*A LAND ROVER pulls up. The QUEEN gets out with her dogs. She notices
PHILIP's struggle with the barbecue . . .*

ELIZABETH

Those fire-lighters no good?
          (carrying tupperware boxes)
I brought some stew just in case. I think it's lamb. We
could always have that cold . . .

No, we'll be all right.

The QUEEN throws some food to her dogs, but makes several hand gestures forbidding them to eat. The DOGS salivate, and whimper, but dutifully show their forbearance. Staring at the food.

The QUEEN, meanwhile, starts setting places at the table with plates, knives and forks . . .

ELIZABETH
Robin had a call from the Prime Minister. Who expressed his concern.

PHILIP turns, an exasperated look . . .

PRINCE PHILIP
About WHAT?

ELIZABETH
The flag above Buckingham Palace. He thinks it should be flying at half-mast.

The DOGS continue to whimper hungrily.

PRINCE PHILIP
Then I hope Robin told him there ISN'T a flag above Buckingham Palace . . .
              (angrily jabs coals with a long, sharp fork)
. . . only the *Royal Standard*, which flies for one reason only. To denote the presence of the Monarch. Since you're *here*, the flagpole is bare. Which is as it should be.

CHARLES clears his throat . . .

CHARLES

Isn't it possible . . . that to *some* people . . . the Royal
Standard is just . . . a flag? And that the flagpole being
bare sends out the wrong signal.

The QUEEN turns. A withering look . . .

ELIZABETH

That's not the point.

PRINCE PHILIP

The point is it's more than four hundred years old. It has
never been lowered for ANYONE . . .

QUEEN MOTHER

Your grandfather didn't get that flag at half-mast when
he died and if your mother were to die tomorrow, *she*
wouldn't get it either.

CHARLES

Yes . . . but sometimes . . . in a situation like this . . . one
has to be flexible . . .

All heads turn. And stare at CHARLES.

CHARLES *(cont'd)*
(shrugs)

It is just a flag.

ELIZABETH

'What about the Union Jack?', was Mr. Blair's next
suggestion.

QUEEN MOTHER
(rolling eyes)

Oh, for heaven's sake.

The next thing he'll be suggesting you change your name
to Hilda and mine to Hector?
          (angry gesture)
Who does he think he's talking to? You're the Sovereign.
The Head of State. You don't get dictated to.
          (a beat)
You've conceded the idea of a public funeral. You've
opened up the parks. That's ENOUGH.

*The QUEEN indicates to PHILIP to keep his voice down, to avoid upsetting
the BOYS, who are still fishing . . .*

          PRINCE PHILIP *(cont'd)*
You wait. In forty-eight hours it will all have calmed
down.

          ELIZABETH
Like those condolence books.

          PRINCE PHILIP
Quite right.
          (a defiant snort)
When we started with one, everyone predicted they
would grow and grow. But we've heard nothing more
about that, see?

CHARLES clears his throat . . .

          CHARLES
Apparently there are now fifteen.

          ELIZABETH
What . . . ?

          CHARLES
And people are queuing through the night.

PHILIP stares. The QUEEN's expression changes.

83. INT. BALMORAL CASTLE—CHARLES'S QUARTERS—
     DAY

CHARLES crosses the saloon to his study, talking to his Private Secretary.

> CHARLES
>
> In one sense it's comforting.
> > *(a beat)*
>
> For the first time my parents can see what it's been like
> for me all these years, being up against her popularity.
> > *(a beat)*
>
> But they're *still* making the mistake of thinking the
> Diana they knew from *living* and *dealing* with her, will
> eventually be the one seen by the public. But it's not. The
> two Dianas, theirs and ours, bear no relation to one
> another at all.

CHARLES looks at LAMPORT . . .

> CHARLES *(cont'd)*
>
> They just *adored* her. Would have loved nothing more
> than for *her* to be Queen.
> > *(a beat)*
>
> Someone *compassionate*. With a *heart*. Gifts in tragically
> short supply around here.

CHARLES looks at LAMPORT . . .

> CHARLES *(cont'd)*
>
> I've been thinking, is the flag flying at half-mast over my
> house at Highgrove?

> LAMPORT
>
> Yes, Sir.

CHARLES

Make sure we get a picture of that in the papers, would you? If my mother wants to make a mess of this, that's her business.

(a beat)

I won't let her drag me down, too.

83A. INT. BLAIR'S BEDROOM—NIGHT

The BLAIRS are in bed working, watching TV. On TV: Tracey Ullman speaks enthusiastically in favour of young, dynamic Tony Blair in London. TONY and CHERIE watch . . .

CHERIE

See? It isn't just me.

TONY

What?

CHERIE

People really DO want change. And want YOU to give it to them.

TONY

And do what? Cut off their heads?

CHERIE

Apparently, one in six people now support the idea of getting rid of the Monarchy.

TONY

(irritated gesture)

That's just the papers spoiling for a fight.

CHERIE

But still, imagine this country without them? With a nice *elected* Head of State?

(a beat)
That'd be some legacy. If the revolution were to happen on your watch.

BLAIR stares. Visibly unsettled.

84.   NO SCENE 84

85.   INT. QUEEN'S BEDROOM—NIGHT

The QUEEN sits at her desk, writing her diary. Her pen scratches across the paper . . .

Presently the PEN stops. She stares for a moment, her face a picture of sadness . . .

                                        FADE TO BLACK

86.   EXT. BALMORAL—DAY

THE SHOOTING PARTY with WILLIAM, HARRY, and several GHILLIES and STALKERS drives off in various JEEPS.

87.   INT. BALMORAL CASTLE—PRIVATE SECRETARY'S
      OFFICE—DAY

JANVRIN stands at the window, looking out as the cars leave . . .

                         JANVRIN
That's the stalking party off?

He takes a deep breath . . .

                         JANVRIN *(cont'd)*
Right, we'd better have a look at these papers.

'Show us there's a heart in the House of Windsor,' says
the *Sun* . . .

His SECRETARY passes a copy over to JANVRIN . . .

SECRETARY *(cont'd)*
'It proves, the Royals are not like us,' the *Mirror*. 'Time
to change the Old Guard at Buckingham Palace.'
Express.

JANVRIN
(heart sinks)
God . . .

The SECRETARY reads from the Independent . . .

SECRETARY
'One can't help wondering whose advice they are taking
for it's clearly the wrong advice . . .'

JANVRIN
Right . . .

The SECRETARY puts down the Independent, *open on a page marked* . . .
'*THE WINDSORS STILL DON'T UNDERSTAND US*'.

JANVRIN's face looks haunted . . .

JANVRIN *(cont'd)*
Well, I'll try not to take that personally.

88. INT. DOWNING STREET—TONY'S STUDY—
     LATE AFTERNOON

*TONY sits on his sofa. The three speech-writing AIDES stand/sit in front of
him. TONY reads from the speech* . . .

TONY

'People have been yearning for a change in this country.'
Good. 'The result is a quiet revolution now taking place.
Led by the real modernisers. The British People . . .'

TONY trails off . . .

TONY

'Revolution'? Not you, too?
                    (trails off)
Who wrote this?

One AIDE puts up his hand.

TONY *(cont'd)*

Where does it come from?

AIDE

Where does it *come* from?

AIDE #2

Just look at the papers. Talk to people on the streets.

AIDE

Something's happening out there.

*TONY's expression changes. He gets to his feet. Walks out, muttering under
his breath . . .*

TONY

Revolution.

The AIDES look at one another . . .

89. INT. DOWNING STREET—CORRIDOR—
     LATE AFTERNOON

TONY puts his head around his SECRETARY's door . . .

> TONY
>
> Get me Balmoral, will you?
>> *(a beat)*
> I'll take it in my office.

90.   INT. DOWNING STREET—TONY'S OFFICE— LATE AFTERNOON

TONY walks back into his office. His face is deadly serious.

> TONY
>
> Right. You lot. Out.

TONY stands by the door. Holding it open. The AIDES stare at one another . . .

> AIDE
>
> What about the speech?

> TONY
>
> Later.

The AIDES file out.

91.   INT. BALMORAL CASTLE—QUEEN'S STUDY— LATE AFTERNOON

The QUEEN and JANVRIN are working in one corner, going through her red boxes. In another corner, PRINCE PHILIP sits watching the television . . .

A tea-tray sits in front of him. Scones. Tea-cakes.

The QUEEN and JANVRIN are finishing off. JANVRIN stands (never sits in her presence) . . .

> JANVRIN
>
> . . . and finally, Ma'am, a DSO medal. A Corporal, in Kosovo . . . you may have read about it in the papers . . . pulled two civilians from a bus after a bomb blast.

The QUEEN signs the certificate of honour. PRINCE PHILIP calls out, indicating the tea . . .

> PRINCE PHILIP
>
> Hurry up, dear. Getting cold.

> ELIZABETH
>
> Is that it?

> JANVRIN
>
> Yes, Ma'am. Just the letter of condolence to the widow of the Ambassador to Brazil.

The QUEEN signs. JANVRIN bows and leaves.

> ELIZABETH
>
> Good.

The QUEEN walks over to join PRINCE PHILIP for tea by the television, when JANVRIN turns (we notice his SECRETARY stands in the doorway) . . .

> JANVRIN
>
> Ma'am, apparently the Prime Minister is on the phone for you.

> PRINCE PHILIP
> *(snaps)*
>
> Tell him to call back.

The QUEEN hesitates, then . . . ever dutiful . . .

>   ELIZABETH
> No, I'd better take it.

PRINCE PHILIP rolls his eyes. JANVRIN nods to his SECRETARY, who rushes off to transfer the call.

The QUEEN walks over to her desk again. Picks up the phone.

>   ELIZABETH *(cont'd)*
> Prime Minister?

92.   INT. DOWNING STREET—LATE AFTERNOON

TONY sits up on his sofa in his office . . .

>   TONY
> Good afternoon, your Majesty. I'm sorry to disturb. I was
> just wondering . . .

93.   INT. BALMORAL—QUEEN'S STUDY—CONTINUOUS

PRINCE PHILIP indicates she should put TONY on speaker-phone. The QUEEN obliges. TONY's voice comes out . . .

>   TONY
> . . . whether you'd seen any of today's papers?

The QUEEN looks at her desk. Most of the newspapers are strewn out in front of her . . .

>   ELIZABETH
> We've managed to look at one or two, yes.

In which case, my next question would be—whether you felt some kind of response might be necessary?

ELIZABETH
No. I believe a few over-eager editors are doing their best to sell newspapers . . . and it would be a mistake to dance to their tune.

TONY
Under normal circumstances I would agree, but . . .

PRINCE PHILIP
(under his breath)
Here we go! The bloody flag again . . . !

ELIZABETH indicates for PHILIP to be quiet . . .

TONY
. . . my advisors have been taking the temperature among people on the streets—and the information I'm getting is that the mood . . .
(choosing words carefully)
. . . is quite delicate.

PRINCE PHILIP
(under his breath)
Of course. That's where all the ruddy cameras are.

ELIZABETH gestures again for PHILIP to 'SSSsshhh' . . .

ELIZABETH
So what would you suggest, Prime Minister? Some kind of statement?

TONY
No, Ma'am. I believe the moment for statements has passed.

TONY takes a deep breath . . .

> TONY *(cont'd)*
> I would suggest flying the flag at half-mast above
> Buckingham Palace . . .

PRINCE PHILIP almost has an apoplexy . . .

> PRINCE PHILIP
> See!

> TONY
> And coming down to London at the earliest opportunity.

PHILIP stares in disbelief . . . 'What?'

> TONY *(cont'd)*
> It would be a great comfort to your people and would
> help them with their grief.

> ELIZABETH
> THEIR grief?

The QUEEN exchanges a look with PHILIP . . .

> ELIZABETH *(cont'd)*
> If you're suggesting that I drop everything and come
> down to London before I attend to two boys that have
> just lost their mother . . . you're mistaken.

> PRINCE PHILIP
> Absurd . . .

ELIZABETH

I doubt there are many who know the British more than I
do, Mr. Blair, nor who has greater faith in their wisdom
and judgement. And it is my belief that they will soon
reject this 'mood' which has been stirred up by the
press . . . in favour of a period of restrained grief, and
sober, *private* mourning.
> *(a beat)*

That's the way we do things in this country. Quietly.
With dignity.
> *(a beat)*

It's what the rest of the world has always admired us for.

TONY

Well, if that's your decision, Ma'am, of course the
government will support it.
> *(a beat)*

Let's keep in touch.

ELIZABETH

Yes.
> *(could hardly be less enthusiastic)*

Let's.

The QUEEN hangs up. Looks over at PHILIP . . .

PRINCE PHILIP

Bloody fool.

He indicates the tea . . .

PRINCE PHILIP *(cont'd)*

Now your tea's gone cold.

94.   INT. BLAIR'S OFFICE—CONTINUOUS

TONY hangs up the phone. He is lost in thought. His SECRETARY sticks her head around the door . . .

> SECRETARY
>
> Robin Janvrin on one.
> > *(a beat)*
> He must have been listening in.

TONY picks up the phone.

> TONY
>
> Mr Janvrin?

95. INT. PRIVATE SECRETARY'S OFFICE— BALMORAL—SAME TIME

JANVRIN speaks on the telephone to TONY BLAIR.

> JANVRIN
>
> Prime Minister, I understand how 'difficult' her behavior must seem to you . . . how 'unhelpful' . . . but try to see it from her perspective . . .
> > *(searches for right words)*
> She's been brought up to believe it's God's will that she is who she is.

> TONY
>
> I think we should leave God out of it. It's just not helpful.

> JANVRIN
>
> She won't have seen anything like this since the Abdication.
> > *(a beat)*
> And I cannot emphasise enough what effect that had on her. Unexpectedly becoming King as good as killed her father.

TONY

All right—but first we have to deal with these terrible
headlines. I'll see what I can do with the Press.

JANVRIN

I'm most grateful, Prime Minister.

TONY

But I can't promise anything. It's not *me* they want to see.

TONY hangs up, thinks, then . . .

95A.   INT CORRIDOR DOWNING STREET

*Tony comes out of his office and walks down the corridor to where the secre-
taries are.*

TONY

Ask Alistair to come and see me, will you.

The Secretary nods and picks up the phone.

TONY *(cont'd)*

And cancel whatever I'm doing tonight.

He turns and goes back to his office.

96.   NO SCENE 96

97.   EXT. BALMORAL CASTLE—DAY

The QUEEN drives out in her Land Rover. And into the countryside . . .

98.   EXT. HIGHLANDS—DAY

The Land Rover shakes and judders. The QUEEN bobs up and down. ESTATE WORKERS remove their hats as she drives past . . .

99. EXT. HIGHLANDS—DAY

The roads have become rougher and narrower. The QUEEN drives with surprising confidence and ability. The QUEEN reaches a fork. She drives on, taking the right fork.

100. EXT. RIVER DEE—DAY

The QUEEN reaches the River Dee, then slows down. She stops and stares. Ahead of her is a difficult, quite perilous crossing.

The QUEEN composes herself, visibly intimidated. A deep breath, then . . .

She drives into the fast-moving river.

101. EXT. RIVER DEE—DAY

The Land Rover's engine roars. The jeep rocks alarmingly side to side as it slowly crosses the river.

One big rock after another. The QUEEN skillfully negotiates the challenge, and is beginning to enjoy the experience . . .

But ahead is one rock she hasn't seen . . .

'Crreak', the Land Rover's undercarriage hits the rock. The ugly sound of tearing metal.

The QUEEN instinctively brakes, then sensing that was the wrong thing to do, slams her foot down on the accelerator. The engine roars in protest, and . . .

'Snap'. An ominous mechanical sound.

ELIZABETH

Oh . . .

The QUEEN's eyes widen. Knowing that sound was serious.

ELIZABETH *(cont'd)*

Oh, you are stupid.

She tries to start the car again, but to no avail. No matter what she does, the Land Rover is stuck . . .

The QUEEN looks into the glove box. Inside is a mobile telephone.

The QUEEN punches in a number . . .

ELIZABETH *(cont'd)*
(into phone)

Hello? Could you put me through to the ghillies' office?
(listens)
Hello, Thomas? I'm afraid I've done something very foolish. I think I've broken the prop-shaft. Crossing the river.

102.   INT. GHILLIES' OFFICE—DAY

The HEAD GHILLIE listens, his expression changes in alarm, then . . .

HEAD GHILLIE

Are you sure, Ma'am?

ELIZABETH

Yes, perfectly. The front one, not the rear. I've lost the four-wheel drive. You forget I worked as a mechanic in the war.

HEAD GHILLIE

And are you all right?

103. INT. LAND ROVER—SAME TIME

The Land Rover creaks as it rocks on the stone..

> ELIZABETH
> Yes, perfectly, thank you. I'm so sorry to waste your
> time . . .

> HEAD GHILIE
> We'll come out straightaway.

> ELIZABETH
> Oh, will you? You are kind. Thank you.
> *(a beat)*
> I'll wait by the car.

*The QUEEN hangs up. Puts the phone away, then opens the Land Rover's
door.*

104. EXT. HIGHLANDS—RIVER DEE—DAY

*The QUEEN gingerly climbs out of the Land Rover, and walks across the
stones to the river bank, getting her shoes wet.*

105. EXT. RIVER BANK—DAY

*The QUEEN sits on a stone by the stranded Land Rover. She sits in si-
lence . . .*

Nothing but the sound of running water, wind in the trees, and birdsong.

Ah, that's good.

*The QUEEN closes her eyes. All around her, silence except for the sounds of
the great outdoors.*

Privacy at last. The first moment of silence in what feels like months. The QUEEN breathes deeply. It's all been a bit much.

No time to think.

One shock after another.

Everyone shouting.

All far too dramatic.

Come to think of it, this is the first time she's been able to . . .

Suddenly, almost imperceptibly, we notice her shoulders are shaking. Not dramatically, but enough to suggest what is happening. The QUEEN—away from the world—is crying.

We only see her back. Presently, she reaches into her jacket pocket, produces a handkerchief, and dabs her eyes. Gradually, she composes herself.

That's better.

Don't want to make a fuss.

The GHILLIES will be here soon.

The QUEEN takes a deep breath. That's better.

Presently the sound of rustling leaves, and the unmistakable sense that she is being watched. Strange . . .

The QUEEN turns to have a look, then almost drops the cup . . .

Standing in front of her, no more than twenty yards, is the STAG.

The QUEEN freezes, hardly dares breathe. It is enormous. His antlers are bigger and more dramatic than she could have imagined.

His fur is thick. His blaze across his nose is distinctive. He is vast, almost the size of a horse.

And staring at her. The QUEEN stares back.

> ELIZABETH
>
> Oh, you are a beauty.

It is unprecedented—almost supernatural. No STAG ever willingly comes this close to humans.

The QUEEN looks into his dark brown eyes. An unmistakable connection between them . . .

It's a magical moment. All around them the whistling of wind, the sound of trees bending. Then, ever so faintly, in the distance . . .

The hum of approaching engines. It's the GHILLIES coming to look for the QUEEN. Sensing this . . .

> ELIZABETH *(cont'd)*
> *(indicating the STAG should go)*
>
> Go. Go on. You'd better go . . .

The STAG remains rooted to the spot . . .

> ELIZABETH *(cont'd)*
> *(claps hands)*
>
> Go. Shoo. Go on.

The ENGINES get closer and closer. The STAG takes a last look at the QUEEN, then briefly inclines his head, turns, and walks off.

No sooner has he disappeared into the woods, than . . .

Several LAND ROVERS appear, driving across the river, and GHILLIES and EQUERRIES jump out, holding tow-ropes, waving in greeting and calling out, concerned for the QUEEN's safety . . .

The QUEEN takes a last look in the direction of the STAG, to make sure he has gone, and smiles to herself.

He's vanished. It's as if he was never there.

105A.   INT. DOWNING STREET—BLAIR'S FLAT—
        AFTERNOON

TONY is putting on a fresh shirt and tie, standing in front of a mirror. CHERIE enters . . .

> CHERIE
> I've just been told there are news crews outside waiting
> for you to come and speak to the people.

> TONY
> Yes.

> CHERIE
> What's that about?

> TONY
> I told the Queen's private secretary I'd do what I could to
> help with the press.

> CHERIE
> Why? Don't you think she deserves it? Sitting up there
> on her 40,000 acres.

> TONY
> I know . . . but allowing her to hang herself might not be
> in our best interests either.

TONY exits, then stops at the door . . .

Besides, I think there's something . . . ugly about the way everyone's started to bully her.

CHERIE watches TONY go.

106.   NO SCENE 106

107.   INT. BALMORAL CASTLE—
QUEEN'S BEDCHAMBER—NIGHT

The QUEEN is in bed, watching television. Staring.

ON SCREEN: television footage of TONY BLAIR, shaking hands with 'the people', defending the QUEEN, helping MOURNERS with their grief . . .

TV PRESENTER
'. . . earlier tonight the Prime Minister went out and pleaded with people to understand the Royals' behaviour . . .'

PRINCE PHILIP appears in the doorway . . .

ELIZABETH
How are the boys?

PRINCE PHILIP
Not so good tonight. A lot of slamming doors.
(a beat)
I think they saw the papers.

The QUEEN's eyes close. Pained . . .

ELIZABETH
Oh, no . . .

ON SCREEN: *television footage of* FAMILIES *sleeping in parks. Kensington Palace is a sea of flowers and tributes. The* MALL *is lined with singing, hugging, weeping* MOURNERS *of all ages and nationalities, holding candles . . .*

PRINCE PHILIP
I'll take them out early again tomorrow morning.

The QUEEN *stares with total lack of comprehension at the* VOX POPS *which the television interviewer is doing . . .*

TV INTERVIEWER (ON TV)
'Where have you come from?'

MOURNER 1 (ON TV)
'Hamburg.'

TV INTERVIEWER (ON TV)
'Hamburg, *Germany?*'

MOURNER 1 (ON TV)
'Well, I just had to be here. She was such a wonderful woman . . .'

PRINCE PHILIP
What?

MOURNER 2 (ON TV)
'She was an angel . . .'

PRINCE PHILIP
. . . and a hysteric.

MOURNER 3 (ON TV)
'So compassionate, and caring . . .'

PRINCE PHILIP
Oh, please . . .

PHILIP indicates the television . . .

PRINCE PHILIP *(cont'd)*
Sleeping in the streets and pulling out their hair for
someone they never knew?

He shoots a quizzical look . . .

PRINCE PHILIP *(cont'd)*
And they think *we're* mad?

PHILIP turns to the QUEEN . . .

PRINCE PHILIP *(cont'd)*
Have you seen the latest funeral guest list?

ELIZABETH
No.

PRINCE PHILIP
I suggest you keep it that way. A chorus line of soap stars
and homosexuals.
(a beat)
Apparently Elton John is going to be singing.

The QUEEN's eyes close. It's agony.

PRINCE PHILIP *(cont'd)*
That'll be a first for Westminster Abbey.

The QUEEN stares distractedly at the television . . .

PRINCE PHILIP *(cont'd)*
Condolence books are now being signed in our embassies
in every major city in the world.
(a beat)
And in London alone the number has reached forty.

After a beat . . .

> PRINCE PHILIP *(cont'd)*
> *(stares at the CROWDS of MOURNERS on the television)*
> This reminds me of one of those films. A few of us in a
> Fort. Hordes of Zulus outside.

A silence. The television coverage continues . . .

> PRINCE PHILIP *(cont'd)*
> So it's VITAL you hold firm. Stick to your guns. You
> wait. They will come to their senses soon.
> > *(a beat)*
> They HAVE to.

PHILIP climbs into bed beside the QUEEN.

> PRINCE PHILIP *(cont'd)*
> C'mon, move over, Cabbage.

*The QUEEN stares at the TV. Staring at a modern Britain, a modern world
she no longer understands.*

108.   EXT. HIGHLANDS—NIGHT

*A bright, full moon. The unmistakable silhouette of THE STAG walks slowly
across the blue-white orb—until he reaches a river . . .*

There, he stops, and bellows imperiously into the night.

FADE TO BLACK

109.   NO SCENE 109

110. INT. DOWNING STREET—BEDROOM—DAY

The following morning.

6:30 am. TONY watches from his bed. The pastel-coloured set of 'GOOD MORNING TV'. The hosts, a MAN and WOMAN in their forties, sit on a sofa. The MAN turns to the camera . . .

> TELEVISION PRESENTER
> 'It's six o'clock. Time for a look at the morning's newspapers. Jenny . . .'

WE CUT TO: a smiling woman in her thirties, who sits at a coffee table which is covered in newspapers . . .

> JENNY
> 'Good morning. Well if you thought yesterday's headlines for the Royals couldn't get any worse—think again.'

111. INT. BALMORAL CASTLE—
       QUEEN'S BEDROOM—DAY

The QUEEN sits in bed, reading the newspapers. Her expression is ashen. She stares at the headlines.

From outside her window, the sound of bagpipes as the PIPER SERGEANT stoically plays in a heavy Scottish downpour . . .

A distant rumble of thunder.

112. INT. DOWNING STREET—TONY'S OFFICE—DAY

8.00 TONY BLAIR is with ALASTAIR CAMPBELL and a team of AIDES are in a meeting room with the newspapers in front of them . . .

ALASTAIR
(takes another paper)
The *Sun*—'Where is our Queen? Where is her flag?'
(takes another paper)
The *Express*, 'Show us you care', with a picture of a
grumpy Queen.
(takes another paper)
The *Mail*— 'Let the Flag Fly at half-mast', and inside,
'The Queen should be here to show her respects.'

ALASTAIR raises his eyebrow.

ALASTAIR *(cont'd)*
Blimey! But the flip-side is . . . 'Blair more popular than
Churchill shock.'

*ALASTAIR expects TONY to be pleased, but instead he appears
concerned . . .*

TONY
Did any of them pick up on our statement of support?

ALASTAIR
Just one.

CAMPBELL shows BLAIR the front page of THE GUARDIAN *where
'BLAIR DEFENDS STOICAL ROYALS . . .' is a minor headline . . .*

ALASTAIR *(cont'd)*
Statements of support don't sell papers.

TONY's expression changes. Frustrated. He thinks, then . . .

TONY
Right . . .

TONY gets to his feet, and walks out. ALASTAIR watches.

113.   NO SCENE 113

114.   EXT. BALMORAL CASTLE—DAY (CLUNY)

The QUEEN walks out for her walk with her Corgis. She has her head-scarf and old raincoat on. DOGS barking excitedly . . .

She is about to set off, when JANVRIN appears, breathlessly . . .

JANVRIN
The Prime Minister for you, Ma'am.

The QUEEN looks pained at the thought . . .

JANVRIN *(cont'd)*
I'm afraid he's rather insisting.

ELIZABETH
All right. I'll take it here.
(a beat)
In the kitchens.

115.   INT. BALMORAL—KITCHENS—DAY

Frantic KITCHEN STAFF disperse in all directions as the QUEEN comes into the kitchen, DOGS barking . . .

COOKS and MAIDS doff their caps, bowing in respect, then run into hiding, as the telephone extension rings . . .

The QUEEN picks it up . . .

ELIZABETH
Good morning, Prime Minister.

The QUEEN gestures to her DOGS. They promptly fall silent.

116. INT. DOWNING STREET—SAME TIME

TONY sits in his chair . . .

> TONY
>
> Good morning, Ma'am.

TONY hesitates, then chooses his words carefully . . .

> TONY *(cont'd)*
> You've seen today's headlines?

117. INT. BALMORAL CASTLE—KITCHENS—SAME TIME

*COOKS and FOOTMEN rush in a chair for the QUEEN, and bring a cup
of tea. The QUEEN sits down . . .*

The DOGS duly follow suit. And sit.

> ELIZABETH
> Yes, I have.

> TONY
> Then I'm sure you'll agree. The situation has become
> quite critical.

TONY takes a breath. Knows this won't be easy.

> TONY *(cont'd)*
> Ma'am, a poll that's to be published in tomorrow's paper
> suggests 70% of people believe your actions have
> damaged the monarchy and one in *four* are now in favour
> of abolishing the monarchy altogether.

Silence.

TONY *(cont'd)*
As your Prime Minister, I believe it's my constitutional
responsibility to ADVISE the following . . .

TONY braces himself. Knows the impact his words will have . . .

118. INT. BALMORAL CASTLE—KITCHEN—DAY

*The QUEEN hangs up. She appears profoundly shaken. She turns to
JANVRIN . . .*

ELIZABETH
Is Queen Elizabeth up yet?

119. INT. BALMORAL CASTLE—STAIRCASE—DAY

The QUEEN walks up a staircase to her mother's quarters . . .

120. INT. BALMORAL CASTLE—CORRIDOR—DAY

*The QUEEN walks along a corridor. She reaches a door. Knocks. Then, rather
touchingly, calls out . . .*

ELIZABETH
Mummy?

121. INT. BALMORAL—QUEEN MOTHER'S BEDROOM—
DAY

*The QUEEN sits on the unmade bed, as the QUEEN MOTHER finishes
getting dressed (attended by DRESSERS) . . .*

ELIZABETH
One—lower the flag to half-mast above Buckingham

Palace and all other Royal residences. Two—leave
Balmoral, and fly down to London at the earliest
opportunity. Three—pay respects in person at Diana's
coffin. And four—make a statement via live television to
my people and the world.

The QUEEN stares.

> ELIZABETH *(cont'd)*
> Swift prosecution of these matters, he felt, *might*, just
> *might* avert disaster.

122.   EXT. BALMORAL GROUNDS—DAY

*The QUEEN and QUEEN MOTHER walk through the grounds: stout,
resolute, waterproofs, rain. A glorious Scottish summer. Distant rumbles of
thunder . . .*

> QUEEN MOTHER
> Obviously you're going to have to talk to the Lord
> Chamberlain about all this.

> ELIZABETH
> I have.

> QUEEN MOTHER
> And to Robert Fellowes.

> ELIZABETH
> To him too.

> QUEEN MOTHER
> And . . . ?

> ELIZABETH
> It seems they both agree with him.

A silence.

QUEEN MOTHER

I see.

The QUEEN stares. Then . . .

ELIZABETH

Something's happened. There's been a change . . . a shift
of values . . .

The QUEEN looks up . . .

ELIZABETH *(cont'd)*

When you no longer understand your people, isn't it time
to hand over to the next generation?

QUEEN MOTHER

Certainly not! Remember the oath you took.

ELIZABETH

'I declare that my whole life, whether it be long or short,
shall be devoted to your service.'

QUEEN MOTHER

Your WHOLE life. That's a commitment to God as well
as your people.

ELIZABETH

But if my actions are damaging the crown?

QUEEN MOTHER

Damaging them? My dear, you are the greatest asset this
institution has. One of the greatest it has EVER had.
The problem will come when you leave, but that's not for
you to worry about—and certainly not today.

The Queen rolls her eyes . . .

Mummy . . .

Then drifts off, into her own thoughts . . .

               ELIZABETH *(cont'd)*
It's just no one seems to value tradition or constancy any
more.
                   (a beat)
It's all about show. About wearing your heart on your
sleeve.

               QUEEN MOTHER
And you're not like that. Never have been. No . . . you
must show strength. Reassert your authority. You sit on
the most powerful throne in Europe. Head of an
unbroken line that goes back more than a thousand years.
How many of your predecessors do you imagine would
have dropped everything and gone down to London
because people holding candles wanted help with their
grief?

*The QUEEN MOTHER's tirade continues, but the QUEEN is not listen-
ing. She knows she has a decision to make.*

               QUEEN MOTHER *(cont'd)*
And as for Mr Blair and his Cheshire Cat grin . . .

123.   EXT. BALMORAL GROUNDS—LATE AFTERNOON

*The stalking party is wrapping up after a day on the moors, some two dozen
people, stalkers, members of the Royal Family, gamekeepers etc. load up the
Land Rovers ready to return to Balmoral Castle.*

A mobile phone rings. The Head Ghillie appears holding the phone.

GHILLIE

Mr Janvrin for you sir.

Prince Philip takes the phone . . . a little surprised.

PRINCE PHILIP

Yes Robin . . . ?

Philip listens.

PRINCE PHILIP *(cont'd)*

What? It's madness! The whole thing! Bloody madness!

Thunderous, Philip hangs up.

PRINCE PHILIP *(cont'd)*

It seems we are going back to London!

PHILIP climbs angrily into the Land Rover, slamming the door. People's eyes widen.

124.   INT. QUEEN'S STUDY—BALMORAL—
        LATE AFTERNOON

The QUEEN's face in close-up. CHARLES peers round the door . . .

He stares. Then, after a beat . . .

CHARLES

I've just been told. You've decided to go back to London.

The QUEEN's face. Avoids eye contact.

CHARLES *(cont'd)*

I just want to say—I admire . . .
                    (strangled, trying to find the right words)
I think it's the right decision.

Silence. CHARLES stares . . .

Let's hope we haven't left it too late.

The QUEEN ignores him. CHARLES goes.

125.   EXT. BALMORAL GATES—DUSK

An explosion of flashbulbs: the motor-winders and flashbulbs of the WORLD's MEDIA whir and pop through the gates of Balmoral Castle.

It's an eerie, venal image. An unmistakable echo of DIANA's world, and her last moments in Paris.

The QUEEN, CHARLES, PHILIP, and the two PRINCES try not to show their hostility, and gingerly inspect the flowers laid at the gates of Balmoral . . .

The QUEEN's face is grim set. Lips pursed. Visibly uneasy with the CAMERAS audibly whirring all around her.

CHARLES holds his son's hand, and tries to concentrate on the flowers and wreaths and tributes.

PRINCE WILLIAM stares at the CAMERAS. Hostile, uncomprehending looks. The beginning of a lifelong animosity. Suddenly . . .

'BANG' a passing motorbike's exhaust backfires. CHARLES jolts in shock, and flinches privately.

Clearly, his fears have not lessened. He's expecting the bullet at any moment . . .

126.   INT. DOWNING STREET—BLAIR FAMILY FLAT—
       SAME TIME

In the kitchen: CHERIE is feeding the kids supper at the kitchen table. The cheery chaos of family life. Everyone talking at once. Laughter. Teasing.

Through an open door, we can see TONY in the sitting-room working. Shirt-sleeves, tie loosened . . .

127.   INT. BLAIR FLAT—SITTING ROOM—SAME TIME

TONY sits with his feet up, doing his boxes, signing papers, and half watching television at the same time.

ON SCREEN: the QUEEN and the Royals doing their photo-call. The voice of the NEWS READER at Channel Four . . .

> NEWS READER (ON TV)
> 'We are just getting some pictures now from Balmoral. These are rather historic shots. Clearly the Queen has responded to criticism that the Royal Family is not engaged . . .'

TONY looks up. Breathes a sigh of relief . . .

> TONY
> *(to himself)*
> Thank God for that.

From the kitchen: CHERIE's voice . . .

> CHERIE
> It's fish-fingers. Want any?

> TONY
> Be right there.

TONY finishes signing the papers. Turns off the TV. Walks into the kitchen. We hear CHERIE's voice as the door closes . . .

CHERIE

I'm afraid they're a bit burned.

FADE TO BLACK

128.   EXT. BALMORAL—DAY

The PIPER SERGEANT walks around the castle perimeter playing the bagpipes.

129.   NO SCENE 129

130.   INT. QUEEN'S BEDROOM—DAY

The Queen is being dressed in black by her DRESSERS. Her face apparently inscrutable. But the difficulty of the situation is clear.

131.   INT. BALMORAL CASTLE—BEDROOMS—
       VARIOUS—DAY

The QUEEN comes downstairs to the first landing where bags are being brought out of the rooms by MAIDS and VALETS.

PRINCE PHILIP

Where are the boys? Have they already left?

ELIZABETH

Yes. They left for London after breakfast. With Charles.

PHILIP shakes his head . . .

PRINCE PHILIP

It's not right, you know.

ELIZABETH

Yes, but further discussion is no longer helpful either.

The QUEEN heads downstairs. PHILIP follows . . .

PRINCE PHILIP

Oh, well. I suppose it gives the ghillies time to find a new stag for the boys now theirs has been shot.

ELIZABETH

What?

The QUEEN momentarily stiffens . . .

PRINCE PHILIP

Haven't you heard? It wandered onto one of the neighbouring estates where it was shot by one of the commercial guests.

ELIZABETH

Really . . . ?

The blood has drained from her face . . .

ELIZABETH *(cont'd)*

Which estate?

132.   EXT. BALMORAL—COURTYARD—DAY

The QUEEN, pulling an old Barbour over her black dress, emerges into a courtyard where the royal cars are being loaded with bags for the trip.

She climbs into a Land Rover, starts the engine.

SECURITY MEN stare quizzically at one another, then leap into life and dash to their own cars to follow.

They drive out of the Balmoral Estate.

133.   INT. DOWNING STREET—BLAIR OFFICE—DAY

TONY sits at his desk working on his speech. A knock on the door. ALAS-
TAIR CAMPBELL enters . . .

> CAMPBELL
> Here's your box. There's some important policy unit stuff
> on top.
> > *(a beat)*
> And you've seen the papers?

> TONY
> *(snaps, irritated)*
> I'm the Prime Minister. Of course I've seen the papers.

ALASTAIR indicates the newspapers laid out on the table . . .

The Times: *'PALACE BENDS THE KNEE TO BLAIR'.*

The Sun: *'QUEEN CAVES IN ON PALACE FLAG'.*

The Express: *'DOWNING STREET STEPS IN TO SAVE QUEEN'.*

The Mirror: *'A QUIET WORD FROM TONY BLAIR AND THE*
NATION GETS ITS WISH'.

> ALASTAIR
> *(in comic voice)*
> 'Your Maj? Come down to London.' 'Who says so?' 'Tony
> Blair.'

ALASTAIR reaches the door—sees TONY. Then . . .

> ALASTAIR *(cont'd)*
> 'Mr Father of the Nation.'

ALASTAIR goes. TONY watches. Losing patience.

134.   EXT. NEIGHBOURING CASTLE—COURTYARD—DAY

The QUEEN's Land Rover, plus a protection vehicle, pulls up in a courtyard at Braemar Castle.

The DRIVERS jump out. Go to open the doors for her . . .

Working STALKERS and GHILLIES stop in their tracks, and double-take. Faces appear at windows. STABLE-HANDS, VISITORS, and ESTATE STAFF stop and stare . . .

We over hear whispers, 'Bloody hell!' 'It's her!'

Presently, the HEAD GHILLIE appears in a doorway, deferentially straightening his hair and clothes. He walks towards the QUEEN.

> HEAD GHILLIE
> Morning, Ma'am. Is it his Lordship you've come to see?

He reaches into his pockets for his cell phone . . .

> ELIZABETH
> No, no . . . please don't disturb him. I've come on another matter. I hope you don't mind . . .

135.   EXT. NEIGHBOURING ESTATE—DAY

The QUEEN and HEAD GHILLIE walk towards a circular cooling room. The HEAD GHILLIE opens the door . . .

136.   INT. NEIGHBOURING ESTATE—
        REFRIGERATED ROOM—DAY

A large cooling room, where the shot animals are washed, disembowelled and cut up.

Hanging in the centre of the room, his innards removed, blood draining onto the floor, is the STAG. A GAMEKEEPER, in overalls, is working on the carcass, when the door opens, and the QUEEN walks in.

The GAMEKEEPER straightens. Stops what he's doing . . .

HEAD GHILLIE

There he is . . .

The QUEEN gasps in shock. Notices the GAMEKEEPER was about to begin the process of severing the STAG's head. The HEAD GHILLIE, mistaking her reaction for admiration, smiles . . .

HEAD GHILLIE *(cont'd)*

Yes, he's a beauty, isn't he? An Imperial, Ma'am. Fourteen pointer.

But the QUEEN has not heard. She indicates a nasty wound . . .

ELIZABETH

He was wounded.

HEAD GHILLIE

Yes. We got our guest in very close, had him lined-up perfect, and still . . .
      (shrugs apologetically)

HEAD GHILLIE *(cont'd)*

. . . an investment banker, Ma'am. From London.

The QUEEN stretches her hand out, almost touches the wound . . .

HEAD GHILLIE *(cont'd)*

I'm afraid the stalkers had to follow him for miles—to finish him off.

ELIZABETH
(voice cracks)
Let's hope he didn't suffer too much.

Unseen by others, the QUEEN's knuckles whiten . . .

ELIZABETH *(cont'd)*
Please pass my congratulations to your guest.

HEAD GHILLIE
I will, Ma'am.

She clears her throat, then goes . . .

HEAD GHILLIE *(cont'd)*
(removing hat)
God bless you.

The QUEEN goes. Dignified on the outside, but dying a thousand deaths underneath.

> *MATCH CUT TO:*

137.   INT. AEROPLANE—ROYAL FLIGHT—DAY

The QUEEN's face. She is staring out of the window, dying a thousand deaths inside, on her way to RAF NORTHOLT in London. She is aboard the private jet belonging to the Queen's Flight, sitting opposite her is the QUEEN MOTHER.

On the table in between them are all the morning's NEWSPAPERS with their humiliating headlines.

A shadow passes across her. The sound of a clearing throat. The QUEEN looks up. It's ROBIN JANVRIN. She snaps out of it.

ELIZABETH

Yes, Robin . . .

She puts on her glasses. Composure returns. Professional again.

JANVRIN

I've done a draft of your television address.

ELIZABETH

Thank you.

JANVRIN puts it down. He notices all the NEWSPAPERS.

ELIZABETH *(cont'd)*

Was there anything else?

JANVRIN opens his mouth, wants to say something to comfort her . . . but realises it would be inappropriate.

JANVRIN

No, Ma'am. Landing in fifteen minutes.

138.   EXT. MALL—DAY—ARCHIVE

The CAR carrying the QUEEN and PRINCE PHILIP sweeps into the MALL.

138A.   INT. DOWNING STREET—
        ALASTAIR'S OFFICE—DAY

ALASTAIR sits at his desk. A TV plays the footage of the QUEEN's car driving through the MALL . . .

A SECRETARY walks in . . .

I've got a copy of the Queen's speech.

She passes it over to ALASTAIR . . .

SECRETARY
Shall I give Tony a copy?

ALASTAIR
Let me have a look at it first.

ALASTAIR starts reading it . . .

139.   INT. CAR—SAME TIME—ARCHIVE /
       RECONSTITUTED ARCHIVE

The QUEEN and PHILIP stare out of the car. For the first time, they get an idea of the actual size and scale of the CROWDS . . .

PRINCE PHILIP
(jaw drops)
Good God . . .

The QUEEN stares in fear and disbelief at the people lining the MALL. In places, the CROWDS are standing twenty deep.

The FACES are reflected in the car windows. Are they hostile? Are they people she understands? Camera flashlights pop.

139A.   INT. DOWNING STREET—ALASTAIR'S OFFICE—
        SAME TIME

ALASTAIR makes a change to the Queen's speech. We CLOSE on the text as he writes, inserting . . .

'. . . speaking as a Grandmother' . . .

In the background, on TV: we see the QUEEN's car pull up. The doors open, the QUEEN gets out . . .

Unaware her words are being edited by her Government.

140.   EXT. BUCKINGHAM PALACE—DAY—LIVE

The QUEEN steps out into the crowds . . .

141.   INT. DOWNING STREET—MONITORING ROOM—
       DAY

TONY and several AIDES are watching the televisions.

ON SCREEN: the QUEEN and PHILIP are looking at bouquets laid at the gates of the Palace, reading messages and inscriptions . . .

Candles are burning. Incense sticks. There are pictures of DIANA, and mini-shrines. Poems have been written.

TONY watches intently. Behind him, the door opens and ALASTAIR enters . . .

> ALASTAIR
> They sent a copy of the Queen's speech.

ALASTAIR holds it between finger and thumb . . .

> ALASTAIR *(cont'd)*
> You might want to scrape the frost off it first.

ALASTAIR passes it to TONY . . .

> ALASTAIR *(cont'd)*
> I made a couple of changes. So it sounds like it comes
> from a *human being*.

ALASTAIR turns, walks towards the door . . .

> ALASTAIR *(cont'd)*
>
> Oh, and one bit of good news. The old boot's FINALLY agreed to pay respects at Diana's coffin.

TONY spins round, eyes flashing in anger . . .

> TONY
>
> You know when you get it wrong, you REALLY get it wrong.
>
> *(a beat)*
>
> That woman has given her whole life in service to her people—fifty years doing a job she NEVER wanted—a job she watched kill her father. She's executed it with dignity, honour and, as far as I can tell, without a single blemish—and now we line up baying for her blood— why? Because she's struggling to lead the world in mourning for a woman who threw everything she offered back in her face, and who seemed, in the last few years, to be committed twenty-four seven to destroy everything she holds dear.

TONY storms off.

142.   EXT. BUCKINGHAM PALACE—DAY

The QUEEN continues to read the hand-written messages for DIANA, 'We love you.' 'Rest with the angels, Diana.' 'You touched us with your love.'

And also some which are downright hostile. 'You were too good for them.' 'They have your blood on their hands.'

The QUEEN stares, visibly shocked, then . . .

Behind her, a small GIRL approaches, holding a bouquet of flowers. She stops in front of the QUEEN . . .

ELIZABETH
Oh . . . hello.

The LITTLE GIRL tries to curtsey . . .

ELIZABETH *(cont'd)*
Would you like me to place them for you?

LITTLE GIRL
No.

ELIZABETH
Oh.

LITTLE GIRL
They're for you.

ELIZABETH
(visibly shocked)
For me . . . ?

The QUEEN is thrown. Suddenly looks utterly lost. Vulnerable, almost child-like. Her eyes are puffy and swollen, as though she is fighting tears . . .

CROWDS of MOURNERS watch intently. The QUEEN takes the flowers, then turns and walks away, visibly shaken . . .

143. INT. BUCKINGHAM PALACE—CHINESE ROOM—DAY

A TELEVISION CREW is rigging lights in the Chinese Room in Bucking-ham Palace. JANVRIN enters and crosses the room. CAMERAS are being fixed to tripods . . .

The QUEEN sits in a corner going through her speech.

JANVRIN
Your Majesty, there's a last minute addition from

Downing Street. They're suggesting adding '. . . and as a grandmother . . .' here.

ELIZABETH

Right.

The QUEEN makes a note on the text . . .

ELIZABETH *(cont'd)*
'So what I say to you now, as your Queen and as a grandmother, I say from my heart.'

JANVRIN

You think you can say it?

ELIZABETH

Do I have a choice?

The QUEEN turns as SOUND RECORDERS fix a clip-mike to her dress.

DIRECTOR

We're ready for you, your Majesty . . .

The QUEEN gets up.

DIRECTOR

Just to confirm this is going out live.

ELIZABETH

Right.

DIRECTOR

And you'll be at the front of the six o'clock news on all the channels.

ELIZABETH

I see.

The QUEEN is led over to where the DIRECTOR has placed a chair and table in front of the cameras and lights . . .

FLOOR MANAGER
(calling out)

Ten seconds, everyone . . .

The QUEEN sits at her desk. Final touches from hair and make-up. The MALL is clearly visible. The QUEEN holds the speech in front of her . . .

DIRECTOR

Five, four . . .

We close on the QUEEN's face, and . . .

ELIZABETH

Since last Saturday's dreadful news we have seen, throughout Britain and the world, an overwhelming expression of sadness at Diana's death . . .

WATCHING FROM THE WINGS:

PRINCE PHILIP and PRINCE CHARLES watch. PHILIP clenches his jaw muscles in irritation.

144.   INT. CHINESE ROOM—SAME TIME

The QUEEN continues . . .

ELIZABETH

We have all been trying in our different ways to cope. The initial shock is often succeeded by a mixture of other feelings. Disbelief, incomprehension, anger and concern for those who remain.

144A.   INT. DOWNING STREET—SAME TIME

TONY and CHERIE BLAIR watch from their apartment . . .

> ELIZABETH (ON TV)
> 'We have all felt these emotions in these last few days. So what I say to you now, as your Queen and as a grandmother, I say from my heart . . .'

TONY flinches in sympathy as she says the line. CHERIE notices this, then . . .

> CHERIE
> 'Heart'? What 'heart'. She doesn't mean a word of this.

> TONY
> That's not the point. What she's doing is extraordinary.
> *(points to the TV)*
> *That's* how you survive.

CHERIE turns, and stares . . .

> CHERIE
> Listen to you! A week ago you were the great moderniser, making speeches about the 'People's Princess', now you've gone weak at the knees.

TONY bristles with irritation . . .

> CHERIE
> I don't know why I'm surprised. In the end, all Labour Prime Ministers go ga-ga for her Maj.

> ELIZABETH (ON TV)
> 'I hope that tomorrow we can all, wherever we are, join in expressing our grief at Diana's loss, and gratitude for her all-too-short life.'

145.   NO SCENE 145

146.   INT. BUCKINGHAM PALACE—CHINESE ROOM—
       SAME TIME

The QUEEN draws to a close. Her face is inscrutable. The DIRECTOR prepares his CREW to wind up . . .

                              ELIZABETH
          May those who died rest in peace and may we, each and
          every one of us . . .

CLOSE-UP OF THE QUEEN:

                         ELIZABETH *(cont'd)*
          . . . thank God for someone who made many, many
          people happy.

The QUEEN holds her expression for the camera. Then . . .

                              DIRECTOR
                             (calls out)
          And we're out . . !

The QUEEN's face relaxes. As does everyone in the room. A huge, collective breathing out.

                         DIRECTOR *(cont'd)*
          Thank you, your Majesty.

But the QUEEN doesn't acknowledge him. She removes her clip-mike, and hands it to the DIRECTOR . . .

. . . then walks over to a waiting PRINCE PHILIP, who protectively extends an arm. The QUEEN and PRINCE PHILIP leave the room. People are left staring awkwardly at one another . . .

OVER THIS: we FADE IN the sound of a haunting, elegiac hymn . . .

146A.   DELETED

147.   INT. WESTMINSTER ABBEY—DAY

A soloist sings 'Libera me, Domine' from Verdi's Requiem, in Westminster Abbey as:

GUESTS (including TOM CRUISE, TOM HANKS, NICOLE KIDMAN, and STEVEN SPIELBERG), arrive with swollen, red eyes, for the funeral.

LUCIANO PAVAROTTI also attends—along with STING, TRUDI STYLER, BILL and HILARY CLINTON, ELTON JOHN, MOHAMMED AL-FAYED, CLIFF RICHARD, QUEEN NOOR . . .

TONY and CHERIE BLAIR take their positions at the front of the church. The First Couple of Great Britain.

148.   EXT. STREETS OF LONDON—DAY

DIANA's coffin is driven away. Showered by flowers all the way to her final resting place at Althorp.

The entire distraught, tearful NATION it seems, has come out onto the streets to pay their final respects.

SLOW FADE TO BLACK

149.   *CAPTION: 'TWO MONTHS LATER'*

150.   INT. DOWNING STREET—BLAIR'S FLAT—
        EVENING

The face of TONY BLAIR stares back from a bathroom mirror. CHERIE is proudly tying his tie. Checking his appearance.

We're in the family apartment above 11, Downing Street. CHERIE puts the finishing touches to his appearance . . .

We notice her appearance has become even more stylish. Gone is her spiky hair. And the rough edges. Every inch the First Lady. They've both come a long way in a short time.

> CHERIE
>
> So? Off to see your girlfriend?

> TONY
>
> Now, now . . .

> CHERIE
>
> I hope she shows you some respect this time. It's quite a debt of gratitude she owes you.

CHERIE straightens his tie . . .

> CHERIE *(cont'd)*
>
> Mr 'Saviour of the Monarchy'.

> TONY
>
> I doubt she'll see it that way.

151.   EXT. BUCKINGHAM PALACE—COURTYARD—
       EVENING

TONY's motorcade sweeps into Buckingham Palace. Doors are opened by his PROTECTION OFFICERS.

TONY steps out to be greeted by the waiting JANVRIN . . .

> TONY
>
> Robin. Good to see you.

JANVRIN
Prime Minister.

TONY
(his most winning smile)
Tony, please . . .

JANVRIN allows himself a private smile . . .

152.   INT. BUCKINGHAM PALACE—CORRIDOR—EVENING

TONY BLAIR and the EQUERRY walk along the corridor, and reach the door.

TONY shoots his cuffs. Clears his throat. The EQUERRY knocks.

153.   INT. AUDIENCE ROOM—EVENING

TONY and the EQUERRY enter. Both bow from the neck . . .

EQUERRY
The Prime Minister, Ma'am.

TONY walks forward and meets the QUEEN, who, like JANVRIN, barely smiles, doesn't make eye contact, shakes his hand, and indicates a seat . . .

ELIZABETH
Do sit down.

TONY
Thank you.

TONY sits, and stares at the QUEEN. Her face is inscrutable.

TONY
It's good to see you again. After quite a summer . . .

The QUEEN's face. Stiffens.

> TONY *(cont'd)*
> I'm referring to your visit to India and Pakistan, where
> your comments about ending historic disagreements went
> down very well.

Silence.

> TONY *(cont'd)*
> And the Commonwealth Heads of Government
> Meeting. I spoke to the Prime Minister of Malawi, who
> was saying how much he appreciated your tough stance
> on Nigeria.

Silence.

> TONY *(cont'd)*
> I meant to tell you at the time but you were being
> monopolised rather.

Silence.

> TONY *(cont'd)*
> I imagine those occasions are quite difficult. Twenty-four
> heads of Government each clamouring for a private
> audience . . .

Silence. TONY takes a deep breath, then . . .

> TONY *(cont'd)*
> Also, we haven't had a chance to speak since THAT
> week. And I wanted to offer my apologies . . .

The QUEEN looks up . . .

> ELIZABETH
> Whatever for?

TONY

In case you'd felt 'manhandled' or 'managed' in any way.

ELIZABETH

Not at all.

A beat.

ELIZABETH *(cont'd)*

I don't think I shall ever understand what happened this
summer.

TONY

The circumstances were exceptional, Ma'am. And in the
end, you showed great personal strength, courage, and
humility.

ELIZABETH

You're confusing humility with humiliation.

TONY

That's not true.

ELIZABETH

You didn't hear what they were saying in the Mall that
Friday.

TONY

I still believe History will show it was a good week for
you.

ELIZABETH

And an even better one for you, Mr Blair.

TONY

But there are fifty-two weeks in a year, Ma'am. And two
and a half thousand in a half century.

The QUEEN looks up. Thrown by his compliment . . .

> TONY *(cont'd)*
> And when people come to assess your legacy, no one will remember those few days.

> ELIZABETH
> Really? You don't feel that what respect or affection people might once have had for . . .

She wants to say 'me', but instead says . . .

> ELIZABETH *(cont'd)*
> . . . this institution has been diminished?

> TONY
> Not at all.

A pause . . .

> ELIZABETH
> I gather some of your closest advisors were less fulsome in their support . . .

> TONY
> One or two. But as a leader one has . . . a different perspective.
> *(a beat)*
> I could never have added my voice to the chorus.

> ELIZABETH
> You're very kind.

The QUEEN looks at TONY, raises an eyebrow . . .

> ELIZABETH *(cont'd)*
> But let's also not forget the more pragmatic reason.

TONY

Which is?

ELIZABETH

That without me there to distract everyone, it'd suddenly
become embarrassingly clear how much unchecked power
the British Prime Minister actually has.

TONY looks up . . .

ELIZABETH *(cont'd)*

If fifty years of doing MY job has taught me anything, it
is that the people doing YOURS generally prefer me with
all my faults to some kind of meddling President . . .
(a beat)
Just look at the French.

The QUEEN opens her handbag, and takes out her reading glasses . . .

ELIZABETH *(cont'd)*

I suppose we'd better get on with the business in hand . . .

The QUEEN looks out of the window. Notices how the sun is setting . . .

ELIZABETH *(cont'd)*

I do love this time of day. Shall we walk while there's still
some sunshine left? I do hope you're a walker.

TONY

I am.

ELIZABETH

Good. The clocks go back next week, then it'll be dark by
five.

TONY and the QUEEN get to their feet.

ELIZABETH *(cont'd)*
I always think these meetings stand a better chance of
succeeding if the Prime Minister is a walker.

FOOTMEN open the door as TONY and the QUEEN go out of the Audi-
ence Room, and into . . .

153A.   INT CORRIDOR

Blair and the Queen come through a door, and emerge into a corridor from the
audience room . . .

ELIZABETH
As a matter of fact, it's how I think best. On my feet. I've
never been one for sitting around endlessly . . . A good
walk and fresh air sorts everything out . . . *(expectedly, she*
stops, and suddenly we realize she's been holding something
back)
One in four, you said? Wanted to get rid of me?

TONY
For about half an hour. But then you came down to
London and all that went away.

ELIZABETH
I've never been hated like that before.

TONY
No. And that must have been difficult.

ELIZABETH
It was. Very.
(a beat)
Ever since Diana people want glamour and tears . . . the
grand performance . . . and I'm not very good at that. I
prefer to keep my feelings to myself . . . foolishly I
believed that's what people wanted from their Queen.

Not to make a fuss nor wear one's heart on one's sleeve,
duty first . . . self second.
                    (pause)
It's how I was brought up, it's all I've ever known.

                    TONY
You were so young when you became Queen.

                    ELIZABETH
I was. A girl.
                    (pause)
But I can see the world has changed. And one must
'modernise'.

                    TONY
Well, perhaps that's where I can help.

                    ELIZABETH
          (with a twinkle as they set off)
Don't get ahead of yourself, Prime Minister, I think you'll
find that I'm supposed to be advising you.

154.   INT. BUCKINGHAM PALACE—CORRIDOR—DAY

*The corridor outside. As the QUEEN passes JANVRIN, he surreptitiously
looks at his watch, and raises his eyebrow. The QUEEN smiles . . .*

155.   INT. BUCKINGHAM PALACE—DOORS LEADING TO
       GARDENS—DAY

*FOOTMEN open double-doors which lead out into the gardens. The
QUEEN and the PRIME MINISTER walk out . . .*

                    ELIZABETH
So . . . what might we expect in your first Parliament?

TONY clears his throat, then . . .

TONY

Well, Ma'am, top of the list is education reform. We want
to radically reduce classroom sizes . . .

*Our CAMERA slowly pulls back over the gardens, until the QUEEN and
TONY are two dots in the distance . . .*

Time has moved on. Sand has covered the footprints.

The momentary hiccup that was 'Diana' already long forgotten . . .

FADE TO BLACK